METROPOLITAN AMERICA

METROPOLITAN AMERICA

Advisory Editor
Richard C. Wade

Research Associate
Eugene P. Moehring

SOCIAL CHARACTERISTICS
OF CITIES

WILLIAM F. OGBURN

ARNO PRESS

A New York Times Company

New York / 1974

Reprint Edition 1974 by Arno Press Inc.

Reprinted from a copy in the
  Newark Public Library

METROPOLITAN AMERICA
ISBN for complete set: 0-405-05380-0
See last pages of this volume for titles.

Manufactured in the United States of America

———◆———

Library of Congress Cataloging in Publication Data

Ogburn, William Fielding, 1886-1959.
    Social characteristics of cities.

    (Metropolitan America)
    Reprint of the ed. published by the International
City Managers' Association, Chicago.
    1. Cities and towns--United States. I. Title.
II. Series.
HT151.04 1974   301.36'3'0973   73-11940
ISBN 0-405-05409-2

SOCIAL CHARACTERISTICS OF CITIES

———•——•———

A Basis for New Interpretations of the Role of the City in American Life

BY

WILLIAM F. OGBURN

Professor of Sociology, University of Chicago

(Director of Research, President's Research
Committee on Social Trends, 1930-1933)

The material in this pamphlet ap-
peared during 1936 and early 1937 as
a series of articles in **Public Management,** official journal of the Inter-
national City Managers' Association.

1937

THE INTERNATIONAL CITY MANAGERS' ASSOCIATION
CHICAGO

PRINTED IN THE UNITED STATES OF AMERICA

FOREWORD

CITIES are the most artificial habitat man has yet lived in. The environment of a city is radically different from that of the farmer and of the hunter, an occupation man followed for many hundreds of thousands of years — long enough to become adapted to it. It is only within the past few generations that significant proportions of the human race have lived in the strange environment of cities, to which they have not become adapted satisfactorily, for the death rate and the crime rate are higher in the city than in the country. They do not breed well in the city, either, for the birth rate is lower there.

But city life is fascinating whether one approves of it or not, and with the economic advantages it offers, men and women leave the farms for the city and will continue to do so until a much larger proportion of us live in urban communities.

The city, however, is not one definite type of community life, for there are varieties of cities — large ones and small, suburbs, factory towns, pleasure resorts, differing greatly one from another. Nor are cities a fixed type of living, for cities, like all else, are changing.

Modern cities are the creation of the railroad, with assistance from the factory. But as the railroad has been supplemented or replaced by the automobile, this new type of transportation, together with the telephone, radio, and moving picture, is modifying the city of the railroad era. Indeed the city as we have known it is being destroyed by these new inventions, and new aggregations of population are being created for which we as yet have no appropriate name but which are sometimes called metropolitan areas. Within these areas are one or more very large cities, several smaller ones of various sizes, some villages, and often a few farms. The inhabitants all read the same newspapers and are linked by a common trading center, and the metropolitan communities are a single area of operations for criminals. Yet there is no single police force for all the places, and no common government.

These same communication inventions are affecting regions as well as cities and making them more alike. Regional differences fade out as isolation disappears. Hence the relation of city to region is changing, for the city dwellers may now come from vast distances. Cities take their personality less and less from the geography of regions. Their differences arise more and more from specialization.

Complexity and heterogeneity lead to specialization, as Herbert Spencer long since showed. It is an age of diversification in occupations. The number and variety are increasing, and each one of us is limiting his work to special fields. Cities do not escape these forces that play upon individuals; they specialize also. Some cities make automobiles, others rubber, or flour, or watches, or moving pictures. Some cities are mainly to sleep in — huge bedrooms, so to speak; others are for widows and older people who no longer work. Some specialize in climate, others offer aid to health or concentrate on play and recreation, while still others are educational centers.

Nor are these all the changes that the communication and transportation inventions are making. The changes in rural life are so rapid and so radical as to be properly called a revolution. They are due not only to the agencies of communication but to the introduction of power machines, not in factories but on wheels and hence suited to the broad acres of cultivated land. The changes in rural life are not without influence on cities, for cities are made up in large part of peoples who migrate from rural regions, often indirectly through small places, to the cities. This movement, however, may not be so conspicuous in the future.

One of the interesting questions regarding transportation inventions and cities has to do with size. The railroads tended to produce huge cities; railroad rates favored large places. On the other hand, automobiles tend to scatter the residences and workshops along the highways and over the country side. Will the big cities therefore grow less in the future or even stop growing and decrease? And will the smaller places grow more rapidly? Perhaps the influence of the automobile and truck on size has been wrongly estimated. Maybe human choices have something to do with it and are as influential as the blind forces of material invention. If so, perhaps these human choices will be based upon considerations other than economics. In this case will people prefer the metropolis as a place of residence or a smaller place? It is possible that there will be a selection of people. The young, unmarried, and childless may prefer the large places, while families with children may want to live in the smaller ones.

It is now 38 years since A. F. Weber wrote *The Growth of Cities in the Nineteenth Century*. There the statistics of urban developments up to that time were explored, but that, of course, was before the coming of the automobile. Many new movements in urban growth have occurred since then, as has been suggested in the preceding paragraphs. These have been studied for the twentieth century and the results set forth in the accompanying chapters. These brief chapters are only the highly distilled results of our statistical laboratory, into which huge volumes of figures and schedules were fed.[1] The presentation is organized around problems rather than being a historical record of development. It is regretted that the picture is not complete, but there were enough data to present the pattern in main outlines. Much more could have been done had resort been made to opinion or to the presentation of mere illustration, but it was felt that the study should be kept in the realm of science, though there are occasional paragraphs of speculation, theory, and interpretation not deduced from facts. The presentation may suffer from having the exhibitions of imagination left in the laboratory and presenting only this bare result, but there is fortunately a gain to the reader in brevity.

The course of urban growth, differentiation, and integration with its environment in the twentieth century is a matter of social forces. Yet it is true that the closeness with which city dwellers live and work together makes possible more collective effort in regard to many matters of human welfare than has been found elsewhere in history, except possibly in the army. Thus it is that some cities have better governments than others, and the governments of some cities do much more for their citizens than do the governments of others. As municipal science develops and is spread through such journals as *Public Management* and other agencies, the possibilities of human effort and choice open up in a magnificent vision. Some of the achievements along these lines are presented in the pages that follow. Since cities are in a flux, there is good opportunity for human will to make application of social science in order to make better places for us to live; and by developments of cities of various sizes and types with differing functions, better adaptations may be made of this new and recent environment to man's biological heritage, which long antedates the days of the cave man and the ice ages.

WILLIAM F. OGBURN

Chicago
March, 1937

[1] The author is greatly indebted to Abe J. Jaffe, Margaretta Reynolds, and John H. Reynolds for valued assistance, and to the Social Science Research Committee of the University of Chicago for financial aid.

CONTENTS

CHAPTER I

POPULATION TRAITS

How do cities differ with respect to the age of the inhabitants, birth rate, sex ratio, number of foreign born, incomes, and cost of living?

CITIES differ in the various social conditions found in them, as, for instance, in crime, church membership, recreation facilities, schools, taxes, death rates, marriage rates, size of family, suicides, numbers of foreign born, numbers engaged in manufacturing, number of artists, rents, and wages. It is the purpose of this study to show in this and succeeding chapters how these and other measurable characteristics vary according to the size of the community, according to their regional location in the United States in 1930, according to their rates of growth and decline, and according to their specialization in particular activities.

The subject is of some interest since we move from one city to another and would like to know in choosing a place to live what are the characteristics of large cities or smaller places and how a city of a particular size in the West differs from one in the East. Furthermore, these various urban conditions are not unrelated to the task of government. Public management is much more difficult under one set of conditions than another. Another point of interest centers around the question of what is the best size of a city. It may be that some cities have grown too big for comfort and economy. The future will undoubtedly see shifts in the sizes of cities. Some will increase, others decrease. This study may throw some light on this question of the optimum size of cities.

This report is confined to matters on which data are available. Consequently it does not pretend to present a complete nor a well-balanced picture. A traveler like André Siegfried would present a different picture. A report from a story-teller such as Sherwood Anderson would be more interesting,

and an account by the poet, Carl Sandburg, might well be more worth while in certain values of life. However, it has seemed desirable to pull together and to analyze the data, readily available, which rest upon fact and not fancy.

A few words of explanation are necessary. In order to deal with the size of cities, those selected for study were classified into nine classes as follows.

NUMBER	POPULATION IN 1930	CITIES
Class 1	1,000,000 and over	5
Class 2	600,000–1,000,000	6
Class 3	300,000– 600,000	15
Class 4	100,000– 300,000	57
Class 5	50,000– 100,000	69
Class 6	25,000– 50,000	69
Class 7	10,000– 25,000	65
Class 8	2,500– 10,000	60
Class 9	2,500 and less	88

For cities of over 100,000 inhabitants all cities in the United States were studied except ten that were suburbs or close to other larger cities. For smaller places each of the samples chosen comprised about the same number of cities from the South, from the West, and from the Northeast. Each class also had approximately the same number from the far West, that is Pacific Coast, but this number was much smaller than in the samples from the other regions. The data are generally for the year 1930.

It is generally known that modern cities have larger proportions of their population of middle age than has the nation as a whole. The cities are thus favored economically, if not in other values. It also appears that the larger cities have larger percentages of the middle-aged than do the smaller cities. The proportions of the young and the proportions of the old in cities of different sizes may also be shown by sizes of cities. To do this, the young are defined as those under 20 years of age and the old as those over 55 years of age. The population in between is for convenience referred to as of middle age. As to the ratio of the number of young to the number of middle-aged, it is smaller in the big cities. For the first six classes of

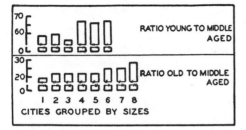

cities, beginning with the largest, the ratios of the young to the middle-aged are 58, 59, 56, 67, 66, 67. The cities of over 300,000 are much alike in this respect but differ from the smaller places, from 25,000 to 300,-000 inhabitants, the different classes of which have about the same proportions of young. In agricultural villages with less than 2,500 persons the young are relatively much more numerous, the ratio being 74. On farms the ratio is even more striking, 116, about twice what it is in the big cities.

This small number of young in comparison with those of working age in the big cities means that the educational burden is less and that not so much of the income of the working population is required to raise children. More money is thus free to be spent on other things. The attitudes in the bigger cities will be more like the attitudes of the middle-aged than of the youth.

As to the old people, there are also fewer of them relatively in the big cities, the ratios to the middle-aged being 19, 22, 22, 22, 22, 25, 25, 28. On the farms the ratio is 29, but in the small agricultural villages the ratio runs as high as 44. Perhaps the middle-aged have moved away from the small villages and old farmers on retiring from work have moved into the village. These differences in regard to the aged are probably more the results of migration of the younger persons than of death rates. Perhaps the

facilities of caring for the old are better in the small places. The proportion of the old in the villages is sufficiently large no doubt to influence the tone of these places.

A suggestion was once made in a journal of opinion that a law should be passed prohibiting children in a large city. However worthy or unworthy that suggestion may be, it is in line with the trends for the birth rate is lower in the large cities than in the smaller ones, as the following number of births per 1,000 population show for the different classes of cities arranged in descending order of size 18, 19, 18, 20, 20, 22, 25. The differences in birth rates would be greater if the cities all had the same percentages of adults of child-bearing age. The large cities now have a rather high percentage of adults of child-bearing age. It is also probably true that the figures are raised for the larger cities because there the popula-

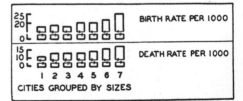

tion is more likely to develop the habit of going to hospitals for delivery than in smaller places. Also prospective mothers come in from the surrounding country and suburbs to have their babies in hospitals. Such a birth is recorded for the city but the residence is elsewhere.

A measure which gets around these difficulties of interpretation somewhat is the number of children under 5 years of age per 1,000 married women 15-45 years of age. The numbers for the cities of the different sizes are 484, 513, 479, 535, 532, 551. The numbers would probably be still larger for towns over 10,000, for those over 2,500 and for villages, if the data were available. On farms the number is much higher, 872, nearly twice as many as in the cities of over a million.

Perhaps the larger cities, with apartment houses and with congested and dangerous streets are not as hospitable to babies and children as are the smaller places. No doubt their scarcity leaves an impression also on the life of these cities.

Death rates are higher in the smaller places, as the following numbers per 1,000 population show: 11, 13, 13, 13, 14, 15, 16. These low death rates in the large cities, however, probably do not mean what they appear to mean, namely that the large cities are healthier, but rather that there are fewer persons of those ages when there are greater chances of dying, to wit, babies and the aged. In any case the people in the smaller places are more concerned with life and death, than those in the large cities.

MEN AND WOMEN

Women like cities, while the work of men is needed on farms. At least such we infer from the ratios of men to women. Among

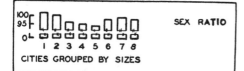

SEX RATIO

CITIES GROUPED BY SIZES

urban populations there are only 97 men to 100 women, while out in the open country there are 115 men to 100 women. How is it in the cities of different sizes? Contrary to expectation, in the very large cities women are not in excess, the sex ratio (number of males per 100 females) for adults being 102 for the cities of over a million, and for cities in Class 2 the men and women are equal in numbers. For the three classes of cities with populations between 600,000 and 50,000 there is an excess of women, only 96, 95, and 94 males over 15 years per 100 females of those ages. The larger proportion of males in the very large cities is probably due to the presence there of large numbers of foreign-born among whom there are many more men than women. In the smaller places, classes 6, 7, and 8, that is, down to those towns of 2,500 inhabitants, there are 98, 99, and 98 men to 100 women. In the small villages there appear to be more men than women, 105 in a sample of 88 agricultural villages, taken in about the same proportions as were the cities from the dif-

ferent regions of the country.

Women seem to prefer the larger cities, as would be clear if it were not for the foreign born. These inequalities in the sex ratios affect the chances of marrying and the standard of living of the people since women are not as productive economically as men. Crime is less prevalent where there are more women. The sex ratio is related to morality and to many other social conditions.

FOREIGN-BORN AND NATIVE WHITE

Immigrants from the farms of Europe and Mexico settle in the largest cities of the United States. The stimulus is probably only in part the factory whistle, for the percentages in factories are about the same in cities of different sizes, yet the foreign-born whites distribute themselves in the following percentages of the population in the different classes of cities arranged according to size: 23, 19, 13, 13, 10, 9, 8, 8. In the villages and in the open country only 3.5 per cent are foreign-born. In 1930 one quarter of the population of cities of over a million was foreign-born, and one-fifth in other cities of over a half million. The American-born offspring of the foreign-born were distributed in much the same manner, showing this distributive process to have been of some duration; 33, 34, 26, 33, 20, 20, 20, 18, 20; and for the villages and farms about 11 per cent.

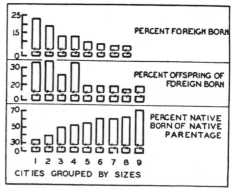

PERCENT FOREIGN BORN

PERCENT OFFSPRING OF FOREIGN BORN

PERCENT NATIVE BORN OF NATIVE PARENTAGE

CITIES GROUPED BY SIZES

The figures for the native-born whites of native-born parents are interesting because of their size. Only a third of the population of cities of over a million inhabitants are of this native stock, while in the villages there are three quarters, as shown by the following percentages: 34, 40, 50, 53, 56, 61, 61, 63, 72, and on farms 68.

This heterogeneity in the large cities is not without significance for politics and the problem of government in a democracy, although crime is less where the foreign-born are most numerous. Even though immigration is restricted or cut off entirely the influence of the immigrant on our city life and voting will probably persist for a generation or more.

INCOMES AND COST OF LIVING

Incomes are larger in the big cities. Perhaps the best evidence is the wages paid, since the great majority of the population who work are wage earners. The estimates as to wages are determined by dividing the total amount paid out in wages in a year, in, say, the manufacturing establishments of a city, by the number of wage earners, as estimated by the United States census. In 1929 in the cities of over a million inhabitants the average annual wages thus determined for manufacturing establishments was $1,570. For other classes of cities, arranged in descending order of size, the annual earnings in manufacturing establishments, similarly determined, were $1,380, $1,300, $1,300, $1,210, $1,190. Wages are thus about a third higher in the largest cities than in the smaller places of 25,000 to 50,000 persons. The lower wages in the smaller places is no doubt one of the reasons why industry is tending to move outward from the big cities to smaller places. The big cities grow bigger perhaps because of the attractions of the great city, but before reaching such a conclusion it is well to note the above observation that wages are lower in the smaller places.

One other source of data on incomes is the annual earnings in retail stores, estimated in approximately the same manner as was the earnings in factories discussed in the preceding paragraph. This series from retail stores quite parallels the one for wages in manufacture: $1,530, $1,400, $1,360, $1,330, $1,310, $1,270, $1,220, $1,250. Stores are not as free to seek lower labor costs as

factories. Hence it is the factories rather than the stores that take the lead in moving outward. Higher wages in the larger cities may be an illusion, for if it costs more to live there the higher wages will not mean much. It is desirable then to examine the data on the cost of living.

It probably costs more to live in the largest cities. Standard articles should not be expected to vary much in price from a large city to a small one. A Ford car costs no less in a small place, nor does a Hart-Schaffner-Marx suit of clothes. There are, too, a very large and increasing number of such standard brands. There might be some differences in food prices, for which we do not have enough adequate data. The item of greatest difference is the value of land, which of course enters into the price of very many articles sold in the cities. Wide differences exist in the values of homes owned as shown by census data for 1930: $7,800, $6,700, $6,400, $5,500, $5,300, $4,700, $4,100 and $3,600 in towns of less than 10,000 inhabitants and more than 2,500. These figures do not reveal possible differences in the qualities of the houses, but they probably mirror differences in the land values. Monthly rentals paid by families not owning their homes tell the same story of higher costs in the large cities. The median rents paid per month in 1930 for the different groupings of cities were $44, $35, $32, $28, $25, $25, and $22 for places of 10,000 to 25,000 inhabitants. The rent is just twice as great in the big cities. Comparing cities of over a million with cities of 10,000 to 25,000 inhabitants, the annual earnings in retail establishments are $310 a year more in the larger places, while the house-rent is $264 a year more.

It may be then that there is still a margin in favor of the large city in income. As evidence, the use of radios may be considered. A standardized article like a radio, many of which carry trade marks, should cost very nearly the same no matter how large the city. Yet in 1930 more families in large cities had them than in smaller places as shown by the percentages of families owning (or paying installments on) them; 59, 56, 50, 41, 42, 41, 38, 39. Do these figures mean that more families can afford to have radios in big cities than in small ones and hence that the margin of incomes over cost of necessities is greater in the large cities? The evidence is obviously not conclusive. Parenthetically, only 21 per cent of farm families had radios in 1930.

There is one other source of data on incomes, the income tax. It is not feasible to determine amounts of income paid by cities, but the per cent of the adult population paying income tax can be ascertained. There are more income taxpayers per 1,000 adult inhabitants in the larger cities than in the small, as shown by the following numbers of income taxpayers per 1,000; 96, 96, 85, 73, 68, 63, 64, 63, 54. This series of the number of income taxpayers roughly corresponds to the series for wages.

Of all the characteristics of cities according to their size, perhaps the one that is most effective generally in determining whether we shall live in a large city or a small one is the size of the income. There are some who argue that the very large cities are too big, that they should decrease or at least not grow any more, while the small places might well increase. The indices of income just presented may be quite inadequate for predicting whether such desiderata

may result, but as they stand income series presented do not seem to indicate, in and

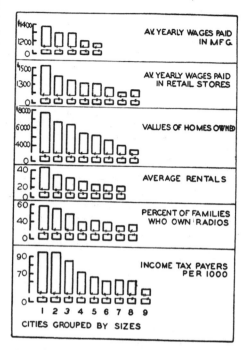

of themselves, that the large cities will stop growing in favor of increases in the smaller ones.

CHAPTER II

OCCUPATIONS

The optimum size of the community varies for any given occupation.
Larger cities have less manufacturing but more clerical occupations.
Crime and religion show striking relationships to the size of cities.

THE occupations we follow, the work we do, occupy a large part of our waking life. Occupations have some influence in shaping our personalities, are important in determining our income and are not wholly unrelated to our happiness. In some cities trade is the major occupation, while in others manufacturing is the dominant type of work. In other cities clerical and office work are very important. In some cities there are more writers, in others more musicians. In small places physicians are scarce, in larger ones there is often a surplus. Cities then may be described in terms of the occupations they provide and an account of them throws light on the conditions of life found in them.

Differences in occupations stand out most sharply in individual comparisons — Flint, Michigan, Hollywood, California, Atlantic City, New Jersey. Such individual peculiarities will be ironed out in averages of groups which only are presented here. Yet group comparisons organized on the basis of size may show some interesting differences. It is the purpose to inquire here whether large or small cities show more or less of this or that class or type of occupation.

THE MAJOR CLASSES OF OCCUPATIONS

The great occupation groupings are agriculture, manufacturing, trade, transportation, clerical work, public service, the professions, and domestic service. The amount of manufacturing carried on in cities of different sizes does not vary much. To measure this cities were classified into six classes according to size.[1]

The percentages of the working population employed in manufacturing establishments are the following for the six classes of cities, beginning with the largest cities: 37, 36, 34, 38, 38, 39. The smaller cities seem to have a slightly larger per cent in manufacturing than have the larger cities. There is a belief that manufacturing is leaving the big cities for the smaller places in search of cheaper labor and land now that the truck makes it easier. But by 1930, at least, the data do not indicate any great exodus from the very large cities. In a sample of very small villages with less than 2,500 population, chosen as agricultural villages, rather than as factory towns, however, there was found to be engaged in manufacturing 31 per cent of the "gainfully occupied" population as the Bureau of the Census calls the working population. In these villages, those practicing the handicrafts would be listed as in manufacturing; and certainly the numbers of employees per establishment would be small. Perhaps by 1940 or 1950 when future censuses are taken there may be smaller percentages in manufacturing in the great cities and larger percentages in towns surrounding the large cities, if not in the villages.

Those engaged in trade are only about half as numerous as those in manufacture.

---

[1] As in the first chapter the following population groupings are used:

NUMBER	POPULATION IN 1930	CITIES
Class 1	1,000,000 and over	5
Class 2	600,000–1,000,000	6
Class 3	300,000– 600,000	15
Class 4	100,000– 300,000	57
Class 5	50,000– 100,000	69
Class 6	25,000– 50,000	69
Class 7	10,000– 25,000	65
Class 8	2,500– 10,000	60
Class 9	2,500 and less	88

While there are undoubtedly cities that are trading centers, the per cent in trade is surprisingly uniform from one sized city to another: 17.1, 16.3, 16.8, 16.5, 15.9, 16.0. In cities of over a million 17.1 per cent are engaged in trade, while for all the cities the average is 16.3.

There is one source of error in these comparisons, due to the fact that in the population census the gainfully occupied persons in a city recorded are only those who live in the city. Salesmen commuting to a store in the city from a suburb are not recorded as being in trade in that city. Hence the occupations having commuters are under-represented in the occupation tabulations for the big cities with suburbs. The discrepancy is probably greatest for those engaged in the professions, in clerical occupations, and in trade. There seems to be no way of estimating the error numerically. The big cities probably have larger per cents in trade than the foregoing figures show.

Wholesale trade is found more in the large cities. Of all those in trade, the percentages in wholesale are the following for the different classes of cities: 40, 41, 35, 30, 27, and 33.

As to those engaged in transportation, as, for instance, chauffeurs, teamsters, conductors, motormen, and in communication as, for instance, telephone operators, one might think that there would be more riding to and fro and more use of telephones in the big cities. But the percentages engaged in transportation and communication in the cities of over a million are not quite so great as in cities not so large. The percentages are 8.3, 9.8, 9.8, 8.7, 8.5, 9.6. Perhaps the volume of traffic per person employed may be greater in the largest cities, or perhaps many engaged in transportation live in suburbs.

The clerical occupations include such jobs as auditors, bookkeepers, accountants, copyists, stenographers. These occupations are found in greater frequency in the large cities: 14, 14, 15, 11, 11, 10. By way of explanation it may be noted that the center of a city with its office buildings operates in matters of control and management, involving a

good deal of clerical aid. The bigger cities thus direct activities in suburbs and nearby cities making use of a large clerical force.

The chief difference with regard to the occupations of personal and domestic service is the slightly smaller per cent in the cities

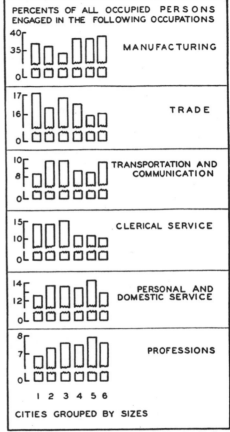

PERCENTS OF ALL OCCUPIED PERSONS ENGAGED IN THE FOLLOWING OCCUPATIONS

MANUFACTURING

TRADE

TRANSPORTATION AND COMMUNICATION

CLERICAL SERVICE

PERSONAL AND DOMESTIC SERVICE

PROFESSIONS

1 2 3 4 5 6

CITIES GROUPED BY SIZES

The bars for the various groups of cities in all charts read from left to right in order of descending size (see footnote on page 6).

of over a million inhabitants. The figures are 12.7, 13.8, 13.7, 13.4, 14.3, 12.9. The villages have 12.7 per cent. It may be that the big cities use more machines and that the small places have more of a family organization to do this work.

The professions are also not quite so fully represented in the big cities as these figures indicate: 6.9, 7.3, 7.6, 7.5, 7.9, 7.6. The slightly smaller per cent in the metropolis is probably due in part to the relatively fewer teachers, who make up a large part of the total number in the professions. There are fewer teachers in the large cities because there are fewer pupils, relative to size. The percentage engaged in the professions would be larger in the big cities if those members of professions who live in suburbs and work in cities were included.

In summarizing, the dividing line seems to come out at the 300,000 population for manufacturing and for clerical occupations, the larger cities having less manufacturing but more clerical occupations. For all other major classes the dividing line seems to come at 1,000,000, the metropolis above that figure having fewer, relatively, engaged in transportation and communication, fewer in domestic and personal service, fewer in the professions, but more in trade.

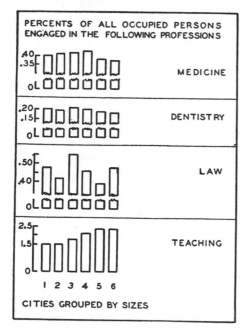

PERCENTS OF ALL OCCUPIED PERSONS
ENGAGED IN THE FOLLOWING PROFESSIONS

MEDICINE

DENTISTRY

LAW

TEACHING

1 2 3 4 5 6

CITIES GROUPED BY SIZES

THE PROFESSIONS

The habits of city dwellers are not shown very well by the broad occupational groupings that have just been discussed. They are revealed better by a less general type of classification, as, for instance, stenographers or chauffeurs. Unfortunately detailed classifications are not available for

all classes of cities. However, there are data for the different professions, which are very interesting. The professions, including doctors, lawyers, musicians, etc., may be viewed in the main as a very high type of personal service found in cultures with a high standard of living.

It is generally known that physicians are scarce in sparsely settled rural counties. It might be inferred then that they are more numerous per unit of population in the big cities than in the smaller ones. The data lend little support for this idea. The percentages of the gainfully occupied persons that are physicians in the six classes of cities are .40, .41, .42, .43, .38, .37. The cities under 100,000 in population seem to have a slightly smaller proportion than those over 100,000. The figures are somewhat similarly distributed for dentists: .20, .19, .21, .20, .19, .18. Again the cities under 100,000 inhabitants seem to have a slightly smaller per cent. Apparently we need only twice as many doctors for the whole body as for the teeth alone. Graduate physicians and dentists probably study carefully their future location and distribute themselves fairly evenly. It is quite possible that they are scarcer in the very small places.

Lawyers, of whom we seem to have slightly more need than physicians, also distribute themselves fairly evenly among the communities of different sizes. The percentages of the working population that are lawyers are .48, .42, .55, .46, .39, .48. One might have guessed that there would be more need for lawyers in the big cities where there are more crimes and presumably more litigation over property, but such does not appear to be the case, when comparisons are made by units of population.

On the other hand the percentages of teachers in the population is smaller in the big cities as the following per cents clearly show: 1.5, 1.5, 1.8, 2.1, 2.4, 2.4. Such a result is probably to be expected since there are fewer children in the large cities. But the proportion of children is only slightly greater and hardly accounts for a proportion of teachers 60 per cent greater in the smaller places. In fact, there are more pupils per teacher in the big cities than in the small ones. This fact does not mean that the smaller places appreciate education more than the larger places, since the latter spend more money per capita for education. Perhaps the larger cities have more educational difficulties to overcome than one of getting enough teachers.

Teachers of music, however, and musicians find employment more readily in the very large cities. The percentages are .60, .48, .50, .54, .45, .43. The most noticeable point about this array is the much larger percentage in the cities of the million population class. We shall have occasion to note that other artists than musicians appear to prefer the metropolis. Perhaps there may be more cultivation of music there. Educational instruction also may be more highly differentiated and specialized.

Artists, sculptors, and teachers of art are also more numerous relatively to population in the larger cities, as indicated by the following series of per cents: .32, .19, .19, .15, .08, .12. Art, as indicated by these occupations, seems to thrive much better in places where there is more than a million population. Perhaps the life there is more congenial to the artist. Perhaps there is more wealth to support art.

A third group of artists are those engaged in writing. Do they thrive best also in densely populated places? The census classification of writers includes not only authors as such but also editors and reporters. Their percentage distribution among the classes of cities is .23, .14, .18, .18, .16, .18; again a heavy preponderance in the metropolis.

Finally, a fourth group of artists, namely, actors and showmen, will be noted. Not all showmen in the census classification are artists but the comparison is probably little disturbed by their inclusion. The per cent distribution of this group of actors and showmen is .43, .17, .16, .18, .19, .19. These data may mean that the cities of over a million give the best support to the theatre.

There has been considerable discussion in recent years over the question of what is the optimum population. So far as the various classes of artists are concerned, the optimum population seems to be over a million.

Religious Occupations

How do religious activities vary in cities of different sizes? The rural church often viewed the cities with their different customs and manners of life as places of iniquity. The pattern of the church in the United States is rural. Perhaps the church should be expected to send missionaries to the corrupt cities, in which case on the basis

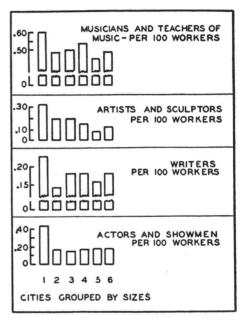

of need there should be more clergy per unit of population in cities. On the other hand, if we assume a lag in adaptation of the rural pattern of the church to city conditions, there would be fewer clergy in the big cities. In fact, the figures show that the larger the city the fewer the clergy, expressed as a per cent of the working population: .18, 23, .26, .28, .34, .34. There are nearly twice as many clergy relatively in Class 6 as in Class 1. Religious workers others than the clergy are also fewer in the largest cities, as shown by the per cents for the first four classes of cities: .07, .08, 10, .10. There is one final measure, namely, church membership. Data on church membership are for 1926 and have been here expressed as percentages of the population 13 years old and over. These per cents show that the smaller the place the larger the church membership: 42, 50, 44, 46, 54, 53. It is clear then that the religious occupations are more numerous relatively in the smaller places.

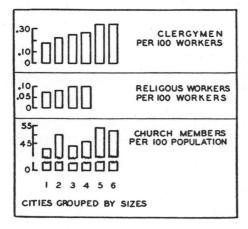

CITIES GROUPED BY SIZES

CRIMINAL OCCUPATIONS

Crime is becoming not only an occupation but an organized economic enterprise. The census takers cannot readily get data on such occupations. But it is possible to put in per cents the statistics of kinds of crime and make some inferences from these as to the prevalence of criminal occupations. First may be presented the data for all crimes taken together. These are the offenses known to the police of the cities in 1934 and include homicides, rape, robbery, assault, burglary, larceny, and automobile thefts. In this case 793 cities have been arranged into six groups divided at 250,000, 100,000, 50,-000, 25,000, and 10,000[2]. The crime rates, that is, the number of offenses per 10,000 population, known to the police are 189, 183, 150, 137, 113, 94. Crime is greatest in the largest cities and diminishes steadily

[2] United States Department of Justice, *Uniform Crime Reports,* Vol. VI, No. 1, First Quarterly Bulletin, 1935, p. 19.

as smaller cities are compared. In such a general crime-rate figure there are so many more larcenies, for instance, than murders, that the rarer crimes are quite obscured. The following table shows the crime rates for the different types of crimes for cities of the different sizes. Robbery is very much greater in the group of largest cities, the rate being about 7 times as great as in the group of smallest cities. Rape has about the same rate in all the different classes of cities. But quite generally crime rates are lower in the smaller places.

OFFENSES KNOWN TO THE POLICE PER 10,000 POPULATION IN 1934 ACCORDING TO SIZE OF CITIES AND TYPES OF CRIMES

OFFENSE	OVER 250,000	100,000–250,000	50,000–100,000	25,000–50,000	10,000–25,000	UNDER 10,000
Murder	.8	.8	.6	.5	.4	.3
Manslaughter..	.4	.4	.3	.4	.3	.3
Rape	.7	.7	.5	.5	.5	.6
Robbery	16.9	6.3	6.0	4.4	3.3	2.5
Assault	4.8	6.1	7.2	4.0	2.3	2.1
Burglary	43.5	43.0	31.3	31.7	26.0	23.3
Larceny	87.0	91.2	83.6	79.0	65.0	49.1
Auto-theft ...	35.2	34.6	21.0	21.0	15.2	9.6

Suicides (committing suicide may be a crime but is surely not an occupation) are almost equally frequent no matter what the size, as the following suicides per 10,000 population show for the groups of cities of different sizes 2.6, 3.0, 2.7, 2.5, 2.4, 2.6, 2.4. Taking one's life seems to be slightly less rare in cities over 300,000 in population but this difference might be removed if the age distribution were the same. That there is not more suicide in the big cities is surprising as the strain of life is supposed to be greater there. In rural areas suicide is about one third less frequent than in cities.

In conclusion, then, occupations are functions of the sizes of cities to some extent. This is notably true of the artist group. The major occupation classes are also slightly different for the very large cities. Crime and religion show very striking relationships to size. The optimum size of a community varies for any given occupation.

CHAPTER III

FAMILY LIFE

One-third of the families in cities consist of no more than two persons.
Large cities tend to discourage marriage and the formation of families.

FROM birth to death we probably spend more time with our families than with any other social organization. Hence we should be interested in it. The family as an institution has been undergoing many changes during the past century and longer. These changes are in general caused by the city or by the forces that have made modern cities. Hence it is peculiarly interesting to observe the characteristics of family life and organization as they are seen in cities of varying sizes, which the reader will no doubt compare as he reads with his conceptions of the traditional rural family.

Curiously, the size of the family household does not vary much from a city of one size to another. The median numbers of persons per 100 households for groups of cities classified according to size[1] and beginning with the largest cities are the following: 321, 322, 315, 325, 327, 323, 322, 318. The first figure on size of family in this array is 321 persons for 100 families which really means 3.21 persons per family on the average, the particular type of average used being the median.

Before discussing why the size of the household is about the same in cities of different sizes, it is desirable to analyze a little further the definition of the family (or

[1]As in the previous two chapters the following population groupings are used:

NUMBER	POPULATION IN 1930	CITIES
Class 1	1,000,000 and over	5
Class 2	600,000–1,000,000	6
Class 3	300,000– 600,000	15
Class 4	100,000– 300,000	57
Class 5	50,000– 100,000	69
Class 6	25,000– 50,000	69
Class 7	10,000– 25,000	65
Class 8	2,500– 10,000	60
Class 9	2,500 and less	88

household) used by the United States Census, from which these data for 1930 are taken. In this connection, a person living alone is recorded in the census as a family. If we omit these one-person families from the calculations and consider as families only family groups of two persons or more, then the median numbers of persons per 100 families in the cities of the different sizes are 339, 345, 335, 345, 345, 342, 343. The size of the household is still about the same from cities of one size to another. A city of over a million has the same size of household, approximately, as a town of 10,000. This is unexpected since the number of persons per 100 farm households is 418 persons, which is 20 or 25 per cent larger than the average household of any of the groups of cities.

COMPOSITION OF FAMILY

It is noted that the foregoing quotations are for sizes of the households rather than for sizes of families consisting only of husband, wife, and children. Included are servants living in the house, relatives, and lodgers. The data on the composition of the family are not given in this detail for the individual cities. But there can be ascertained the percentage of all households that have lodgers. These per cents for the different sizes of cities are 14, 13, 12, 12, 12, 11, which show that the larger cities have more lodgers. There are more hotels in big cities than in small, but there are also more families taking in lodgers. The household of the old-time rural family consisted, besides the members of the family, of workers on the farms and helpers in the various economic duties of the home, and was large because of these duties. Some households of the modern city are large because they afford, not economic opportunities for workers, but a resting place for roomers. In the open country,

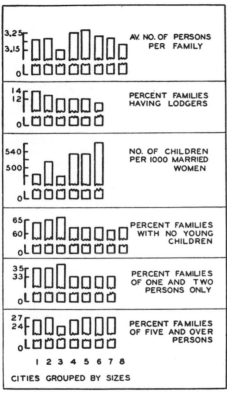

AV. NO. OF PERSONS PER FAMILY

PERCENT FAMILIES HAVING LODGERS

NO. OF CHILDREN PER 1000 MARRIED WOMEN

PERCENT FAMILIES WITH NO YOUNG CHILDREN

PERCENT FAMILIES OF ONE AND TWO PERSONS ONLY

PERCENT FAMILIES OF FIVE AND OVER PERSONS

1 2 3 4 5 6 7 8

CITIES GROUPED BY SIZES

The bars for the various groups of cities in all charts read from left to right in order of descending size (see footnote on page 11).

though, where there are no hotels, the per cent of farms with lodgers is only eight, an interesting comment on the difference between city and country. Farming is still a family occupation, though transient labor and the growth of commercial farming are changing it.

If, then, it were possible to subtract the number of lodgers from the size of the household, the family in the big city would probably be found smaller than in other cities, towns, and villages. This inference is strengthened by the statistics on the ratio of children under 5 years of age to the

number of married women 15 to 45 years of age. The numbers of such young children per 1,000 married women of these ages are, for the different sized cities, 484, 514, 479, 535, 532, 562. On farms the number is 872, nearly twice as many as in cities of over a million.

That there are fewer children in large cities is evidenced by data showing the number of families with no children under 10 years of age living at home. In the big cities nearly two-thirds of all families have no children under 10 years of age. The per cents for the different classes of cities are the following: 64, 65, 66, 62, 62, 62, 61, 62. On farms the per cent is 57. These conclusions are checked by other data on size of family. The percentage of families consisting of no more than two persons is larger in the large cities, the percentages being 35, 35, 36, 33, 33, 33, 33 for the different classes of cities. About one-third of the families thus consist of no more than two persons. On farms only one-fourth of the families are of this small size. On the other hand, families of five or more persons are less numerous in the large places, as shown by the following per cents: 26, 27, 24, 26, 27, 27, 27. On farms nearly half, 42 per cent, of all families have five or more persons in them.

In summary, the size of the household is about the same in large cities as in small, because of the presence of more roomers in the households of the larger cities. The family proper is a bit smaller in the large cities because of a slightly lower birth rate. Why the birth rate is lower is, of course, another story. The large cities resemble the small ones in family much more closely than the small towns resemble the farms.

MARRIAGE

Every person is born into a family, but not every one forms a new family. The time for forming families is in the twenties. After 30 years of age, not many single women marry to form a family. Most men who are going to marry have married by 35 years of age. With men, the larger the city the larger the proportion of young men who have never married. The percentages of young men 20 to 35 who have never married are 18, 18, 16, 15, 15, 14 for classes of cities of different sizes.

Not so many young women of these ages are single, for the age of marriage of females

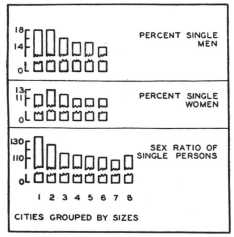

is younger, perhaps for both biological and economic reasons. Also, the differences in the percentages of single women from city to city is not so great, as the following percentages of single women of these ages show: 12, 13, 12, 11, 11, 11.

The larger cities seem to encourage the single life more than other cities. On farms only 8 per cent of the young women of these ages are single, while 14 per cent of the young men are single.

The proportion of men married depends on the number of available women and likewise the number of women married depends somewhat on the supply of men. Some idea of this relationship may be measured by the number of single males over 15 years of age to 100 single females of these ages. The numbers are 136, 127, 117, 115, 114, 112, 109, 115. This high excess of single men over single women in the very large cities may be due in part to the congregation of immigrants in larger cities, among whom there are more males than females who have crossed the ocean to seek a new home. These large numbers of unmarried in the big cities and the excesses of single men over single women no doubt have various social consequences. Crime is more frequent among men

than women and among single men than married men. The death rate is also greater among single men than married men, as is also the insanity rate.

Although the percentage of the young persons unmarried increases as the city gets larger, the percentage of the adult population (that is, those over 15 years of age) that are married is very nearly the same in the large cities as in the small: 59, 56, 59, 60, 60, 60, 60, 59. This is to be explained by the fact that the large cities have a greater proportion of middle-aged persons— the group containing the highest proportion of married persons as indicated in the first article in this series. Even without taking into consideration the age distribution, the average percentage married in cities of over 300,000 is 58, while for cities of lesser size it is 60. If the age distributions were the same, the differences in percentages of married persons would be even more noticeable. There is a large number of the offspring of the foreign-born in large cities, although a

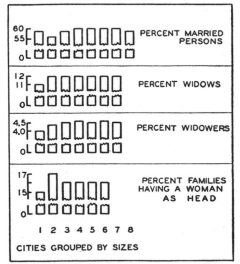

lower percentage married, for not as many of the children of immigrants marry as do the general population.

We conclude, then, that the large cities tend to discourage marriage and the formation of families. There may be an economic factor in the explanation, since, from a man's point of view, so many economic services rendered by a wife may be purchased elsewhere in large cities, as cooked food in restaurants, sewing, and laundering, that marriage becomes less necessary on these grounds.

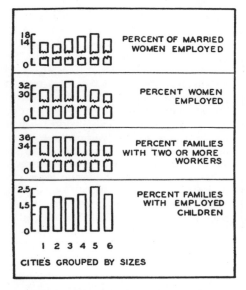

PERCENT OF MARRIED WOMEN EMPLOYED

PERCENT WOMEN EMPLOYED

PERCENT FAMILIES WITH TWO OR MORE WORKERS

PERCENT FAMILIES WITH EMPLOYED CHILDREN

1 2 3 4 5 6

CITIES GROUPED BY SIZES

After families are formed, they become broken by death as the parties to the marriage contract become older. Those who do not remarry after the death of a mate remain as widows and widowers. There are fewer widows and widowers in the very large cities. If the age distribution were the same for cities of different sizes, this differential would be lessened and perhaps reversed. But in any case, there appear to be fewer widows in the very large places, as shown by the following percentages of the adult population over 15: 11, 12, 12, 12, 12, 12, 12, and certainly fewer widowers as shown by the following percentages: 4.0, 4.4, 4.5, 4.6, 4.5, 4.6, 4.5. On the farms there are more widowers, 4.8 per cent, but fewer widows, 8.1 per cent, than in the cities. It is interesting to note that the percentages of families with a woman head run rather high: 15, 17, 16, 16, 16, 16. On farms, only 6 per cent have a woman head. It is observed, parenthetically, that the widows are more than twice as numerous as widowers, yet there is very little difference in the death rate of men and

women. Widowers, therefore, must remarry more than widows.

EMPLOYMENT

For a century steam power has been taking the traditional occupations of women away from the home and putting them in the factory; yet women have not followed their occupations away from home, partly, no doubt, because childbearing and child rearing kept them at home. But in 1930 one in 8 or 9 married women of the cities was employed away from home. One might guess that there would be more married women employed in the big cities, since the birth rate is lower, and since there are fewer children under 10 years of age. But such is not the case, as the following percentages of married women indicate: 14, 13, 16, 17, 18, 16, excluding southern cities where large numbers of Negro women are employed, lowering the percentages but not changing the differentials much. In explanation of why larger cities have fewer married women employed as compared with smaller cities, it is quite possible that the jobs available for women are taken by the unmarried, who migrate to the cities, and that by holding jobs they retard their marriage. Some support of this view is furnished by the percentages of females, 15 years old and over, who are employed: 31, 32, 33, 32, 31, 30. The percentage of females employed is slightly larger in the large cities over 300,000.

Members of the family group other than the husband and wife may be employed away from home also. The families with more than one gainful worker are about twice as numerous as families with a married woman employed. The per cents of all families with more than one gainful worker are 35, 36, 36, 35, 35, 34. Perhaps these figures show a slight tendency for more members of the family to work in the larger cities. So large a number of families with more than one worker contributes somewhat to break the shock of unemployment. Sometimes the other gainful workers in families are children. The percentages of families with children (10 to 15 years of age) at work nowadays are small but somewhat greater in the smaller cities, as the following percentages show: 1.4, 2.0, 1.9, 2.2, 2.6, 2.2. The reason why there is less child labor in the big cities is not known. It is interesting to note in regard to these statistics on family activities how frequently the dividing line is at cities with a population of 300,000, and not one million or 100,000.

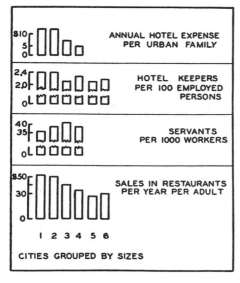

ECONOMIC FUNCTIONS

In the past the family performed many economic functions from spinning to making soap. Most of these functions have left the home for the factory. Sometimes the extent that these activities are carried on outside the family affords an index of family change. Thus if the larger cities showed a larger amount of laundry done outside homes in laundries, than did smaller cities, the inference would be that this economic function of laundering had been transferred from home to factory to a greater extent in the metropolis. Hence it might be argued that the family had disintegrated or evolved further than in the smaller places. It is the purpose here to examine a few such indices for which data are available.

Hotels may symbolize a diminished family, particularly if they are residence hotels. The dollars per family spent in hotels where occupancy is mainly permanent are as follows for the first four groups of cities: $12, $12, $7, $5. The per capita annual sales in eating places outside the home also decrease as the cities decrease in size, as the following amounts show: $52, $50, $40, $34, $28, $30. The apartment house usually means slightly fewer economic family functions, since apartments are smaller than homesteads and janitor services are often supplied outside the family. Multi-family dwellings are more numerous in larger cities, as the following percentages of family dwellings containing more than two families show: 10, 9, 7, 5, 4, 3, 2, 2.

The number of domestic servants would seem to be correlated with the extent of home activities, though there may be several qualifications. Servants are slightly fewer in the large cities, as measured by the numbers per 1,000 gainfully occupied: 36, 38, 41, 38. The employment of domestic servants is a function of wealth in modern cities, and perhaps of size of families. The use of household machines also increases technolog-

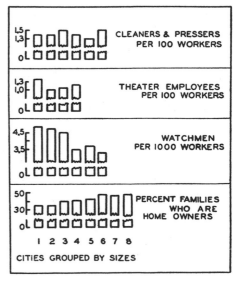

ical unemployment among domestic servants.

Electricity is the power behind most household machines. Electricians are slightly more numerous in the bigger cities as measured in per cents of the working population: .84, .70, .72, .68, .67, .74. The use of electricians may also be a function of income.

Cleaning, dyeing, and pressing are being done more away from home, but the percentages employed in these industries are much the same from one sized city to another, to wit: 1.4, 1.4, 1.5, 1.4, 1.3, 1.5. There are probably more commercial amusements to entice members of the family away from home in the large cities than in the small cities, but to show it would require data on a large list of recreations. Theatre managers, owners, and workers are more numerous in the large city as shown by the following per cents: 1.4, 1.0, 1.1, 1.2. There are also many more actors in the bigger cities.

In early times the head of the family was supposed to protect the wife and children. This he did with his sword or gun. Now, protection has shifted to police and guards. There are, as will be shown in the fourth article of this series, more police relatively in the big cities. The number of guards and watchmen per 1,000 of the working population is greater also in the metropolis, the numbers being 4.8, 4.7, 4.5, 3.5, 3.7, 3.3. Most of these, no doubt, guard property away from the home. The family no longer keeps sole guard over its property.

The traditional family in the United States probably owned its home, though such was not the case among the rural peasantry of other countries. Farm tenantry has increased greatly in this country, so that in 1930 only 53 per cent of the farmers owned their homes. The percentage of home owners in cities is not so great, and the larger the city the smaller the percentage of home owners, as the following per cents show: 36, 36, 40, 41, 43, 48, 47, 48. In the agricultural villages 61 per cent of families own their own homes. Home ownership is supposed to carry with it certain virtues and valuable qualities of character; it is therefore impressive to discover such small percentages of home owners.

In these brief considerations of the loss of family functions, the indications are that families in the very large cities have lost more of these functions than families in smaller places. The inquiry here has not been extensive enough for want of data, but it is strongly suggestive.

In conclusion, then, the pattern of family life and organization from which modifications have increasingly occurred is the rural type. The village family is somewhat different; the family in the small city, more so, but there are some exceptions to this direction of change. The family in the great metropolis has changed the most.

CHAPTER IV

THE SOCIAL SERVICES

The cities over one million population spend three times more per capita for health services than cities of 30,000 to 50,000, but there is only slight difference in the cost of education.

THE government of cities is characterized by the number and variety of functions it performs. It touches the lives of the people in more intimate ways than the government of any other unit. It not only furnishes protection through the fire department, the police, and the courts, but it paves our streets, educates our children, collects garbage, determines what type of house may be built, provides recreation, lends us books to read, and sees that we do not get cheated in weight on purchases.

The county government never did all these services, partly because the farm families do them for themselves and partly because the families were so scattered that it was impractical or unnecessary. But when people live in cities, the family loses many of its functions and the city government has to take them over. The crowded living conditions made governmental provisions and regulations necessary. Finally with the increased wealth accumulated in cities it was possible to add new services which a higher standard of living makes possible. So then, the city government has grown to do many things for reasons inherent in the evolution of social institutions and in the necessary shifting of functions from one organization to another.

How do cities of different sizes compare in the extent of such social services rendered to their populations? Does the large city perform more of these functions than the small one? And does the citizen have to pay more taxes for such services in the large cities? The most extensive data available on this subject are the comparative costs for these functions. In using this criterion of costs, it may be argued that costs measure only waste or economy and not amount. But for a large number of cities these different practices in economical or wasteful bureaus will be averaged out for a class of cities of a given size. Furthermore, it may be argued that if, say, libraries cost more per capita to a large city government than to a small one, it may not mean that there are more libraries or more books loaned but rather that it costs more to run a library of a given size in a big city than in a small one, for salaries and other costs may be higher. But if the amount spent on libraries is two or three times greater per capita in a big city than in a small one, the whole of this difference could hardly be accounted for by differences in salaries and prices in the two places.

CHARITIES AND CORRECTIONS

A field of governmental activity in cities is that of charities and corrections, as the terminology of a generation ago described it. It means the care of the poor in and outside of institutions and the support of hospitals. The corrections are for both minors and adults and include probation work also. To measure the activity of city government in this field cities are classified into six groups according to size, the dividing lines being at 1,000,000; 600,000; 300,000; 100,000; 50,000; and 30,000.[1] For the last three groups only samples of 50 or 60 cities each are used. The annual costs per capita of such public

[1] This classification is slightly different from that used in the three previous chapters.

charities in the six classes of cities are $4.80, $4.70, $4,60, $1.70, $1.40, $1.50.[2] There is quite a difference between the per capita costs for cities above 300,000 and those below. This is due to the fact that so few of these cities under 300,000 support hospitals and corrections. This work is handled by

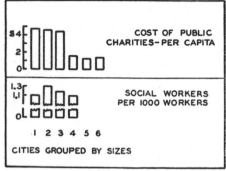

The bars for the various groups of cities in all charts read from left to right in order of descending size (see page 17 for population groups).

other governmental agencies for these smaller cities. The figures do not represent the per capita amounts spent by governments in these communities but only that spent by municipal governments. If, however, hospitals and corrections are omitted, leaving only the care of the poor in institutions, the per capita costs are larger in the larger cities; $0.70, $0.50, $0.57, $0.51, $0.70. (The first item is for cities over 500,000 and the second for cities between 500,000 and 300,000. The other classes are the same as formerly used, though the cities are different. The cities around 50,000 to 30,000 have a high figure because care of poor in hospitals is included under care of poor, while in larger cities it is included under hospitals, which are omitted from the above figures.) The foregoing figures, then, show simply the load in this field carried by municipal governments. This charitable and correctional activity is probably greater in the large cities, since the family organization carries more of the load in the smaller places, as probably does private charity also.

2 These data and most of those which follow are taken from *Financial Statistics of Cities for 1930*, published by the United States Bureau of the Census.

The number of social workers, many of whom are engaged in charitable undertakings, per 1,000 employed is about the same for the first four classes of cities, 1.1, 1.3, 1.2, 1.1. Unfortunately data for cities under 100,000 are not available. Perhaps there may be fewer. The number of religious workers per 1,000 employed seems to increase as the city becomes smaller, as the following figures show: .7, .8, 1.0, 1.0. The proportion in cities of less than 100,000 inhabitants is not known.

CONSERVATION OF HEALTH

Good health is probably more difficult to maintain in the very large cities. The dangers of infection and contagion need to be watched very closely. Under conservation of health are included the prevention and treatment of communicable diseases, medical work among school children, conservation of child life, food regulation and inspection, and the keeping of records of vital statistics. The municipal expenditures per capita for the preservation of health are about three times as great in the cities with more than a million inhabitants as in cities of 30,000 to 50,000 persons. The costs per capita per year are $1.50, $1.40, $1.60, $0.90, $0.60, $0.50. It is doubtful if a person in the large city is three times as healthy as a person in the small one. Indeed, with all the

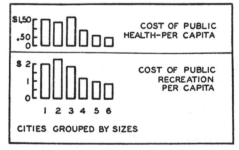

expenditure on health in cities, the death rate is higher than on farms, where the community expenditure for health is almost nothing.

RECREATION

Recreation seems to cost more in cities than in the country. Big cities appear to have more private agencies selling recreation for a price than do the smaller cities. The government provides some recreation for the people, mainly in parks, boulevards, and playgrounds, but sometimes in concerts and various small miscellaneous items. The municipal budgets contain larger items providing recreation for people in the very large cities than in the smaller ones. The annual per capita costs are $2.00, $2.30, $1.90, $1.20, $1.00, $0.90. The question is naturally raised as to whether people in the larger places need more recreation, whether they have more money to pay for it, or whether the price is higher. Play space in parks is certainly more needed in the large cities.

EDUCATION

Educating children is the most expensive of the social services. Like the other governmental functions discussed, the governmental expenditure for schools per adult over 21 years of age is more in the larger cities, but only slightly more, as shown by the following annual costs: $26, $24, $25, $23, $22, $22. The differentials between cities of different sizes are much less than in the case of charities, health, and recreation. There are fewer children per adult to send to school, though, in the very large cities. If the costs be reckoned per young person 7 to 20 years of age, the differentials between cities of different sizes are somewhat greater: $102, $94, $97, $79, $77, $73. The bigger cities may get more or better schooling for their money outlay, and then they may not. If the number of pupils per teacher be used as a criterion, it would appear that the smaller cities have the better schools. The pupils per teacher were determined by dividing the total school attendance by the number reported as following the occupation of teacher. They are the following: 29, 29, 24, 25, 22, 22. On the other hand there appear to be no larger percentages of children of high school age in school in the small places than in the larger ones. Taking the ages 16 and 17 as a criterion, the percentages of children of these ages in school in cities of different sizes are 62, 58, 63, 60, 60, 63. For places of 10,000 to 25,000 population the

per cent attendance is 64 and in the villages 73. The very high percentage of attendance in villages under 2,500 is probably due to the presence of youths from the farms, who are recorded as attending village schools but who are reported as living on farms. On farms the percentage of boys and girls of 16 and 17 years of age attending school is 52.

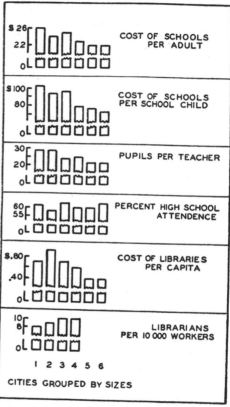

The greater costs of education in the larger cities may be due to higher prices there. Also it is possible that in the smaller places the families may perform some services which the schools render in large places, as, for instance, teaching of home economics or manual training.

LIBRARIES

The governments of large cities spend more on libraries than do the governments of the smaller cities, the per capita costs being $0.70, $0.90, $0.70, $0.60, $0.40, and

$0.40. There is some doubt as to whether these figures mean better or more library service, since the differentials in costs are not great, and also since the number of librarians is relatively no greater in the large cities. The United States Census of occupations records for the first four classes of cities slightly smaller percentages of librarians in the larger cities. The number of librarians per 10,000 persons employed is: 8, 9, 10, 10 for these four classes of cities. Data are not available for smaller places. Book circulation statistics, not readily available, would throw light on this question.

COURTS AND POLICE

It is more difficult to control human behavior in large cities where the social pressure and gossip, found in small places with a Main Street, are not as effective. Hence, it is to be expected that policing and courts will cost more. The city courts deal mainly with the smaller offenses. The per capita costs of the police courts of the cities of different sizes are $0.60, $0.40, $0.20, $0.15, $0.10, $0.10.

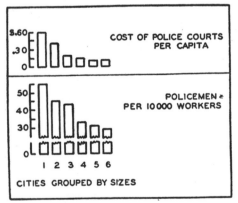

There are also more police relatively in the larger cities. The number of policemen per 10,000 persons employed in the various groups of cities classified according to size is: 55, 45, 43, 33, 31, 29. Whether traffic problems account for the extra police is difficult to say.

Evidently, then, the problem of regulating conduct in those matters covered by city ordinances is greater in the larger cities than in the smaller ones. Perhaps if the court costs for major offenses which are handled by state and county courts could be allocated between cities and rural regions, the handling of court cases from the large cities would be even more costly, relative to the smaller places.

PUBLIC SERVICE ENTERPRISES

Many cities go into the business of selling their citizens certain commodities or services which are paid for in the main not by general taxes but by receipts from citizens making the purchases. In general these are from the classes of business called public utilities. Thus practically all cities sell water to their inhabitants, many provide market places, only a few own electric light and power systems, a few rent halls and auditoriums, many have municipal docks. A total of all such revenues divided by the population will give some rough indication of the extent to which cities of the different sizes have gone into the field of running public utilities. The per capita receipts from the earnings of public service enterprises is larger in the big cities, as shown by the following figures: 11, 8, 8, 6, 6, 8. The big cities are more highly organized and differentiated, and it is perhaps not surprising that the governments of the metropolises should go in for more public utility enterprises.

TOTAL COSTS OF GOVERNMENT

All of the costs of the social services supplied by governments that have been presented are greater per capita in the large cities than in the small ones. Without going more into detail, we may summarize all the cost payments of the governments and compare the cities by sizes. It is not surprising, then, that the total costs of governments are larger in the big cities, as shown by the following annual per capita cost payments for the different classes of cities: $104, $98, $88, $60, $54, $51. The cost of city government per citizen is about twice as great in cities of over a million as in cities from 30,000 to 50,000. Governmental cost payments include funds for maintenance and operation, as well as interest and outlays. It includes, therefore, properties being constructed or purchased and public·improvements being built or acquired.

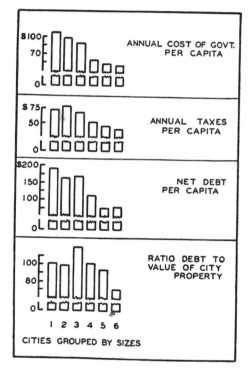

Taxes

The total costs of city governments are therefore larger than the funds raised from taxes, since total costs include special assessments and charges and expenditures from borrowed funds. By taxes are meant general property taxes, poll tax, special taxes, and licenses. The course of taxes, however, should resemble the course of governmental costs from large places to small. The per capita taxes show they do: $72, $78, $68, $51, $45, $41. The per capita taxes are nearly twice as great in the Class 1 cities as in those of Class 6. The tax burden is greater, but perhaps the service bought by the taxes is also greater.

Debt

The great cities not only cost more to run each year than the smaller cities, but in order to get the plant and equipment they possess, they have had to go deeper in debt, as the indebtedness per capita shows: $188, $166, $169, $113, $75, $77. These debt figures are for the net debt, that is, funded and floating debt less assets in general sinking funds. Debt may be evaluated not only as the amount each inhabitant owes, but it may also be expressed as a fraction of the total value of property owned by a city. On this basis the cities under 100,000 in population are better off than the bigger cities. Also it is Class 3, with cities from 100,000 to 300,000, that has the greatest debt, as is shown by the following percentages: 101, 98, 119, 101, 94, 70.

In conclusion it may be recalled that very sparsely settled regions have not enough population nor enough wealth to provide the social services such as schools, libraries, and hospitals. We already know, however, that cities can and do provide them. Now, it is known from the foregoing study that the cities of greatest size generally provide more of such services than do the smaller places. Density of population, then, seems to be correlated straight through with the provision of social services.

CHAPTER V

DAILY LIVING

An analysis of the differences in the activities of people living in various sized cities shows that the larger cities present more opportunities than the smaller places.

WE CAN see a big-league ball game only in a large city, and we cannot go to the opera in a small place. But not many of the customs of daily living have been recorded so that comparisons can be made from one city to another. However, it is known that we are more likely to live in apartment houses in large cities and that there is more yard space for the home in smaller cities. There is a wider selection of women's clothing to be purchased in the metropolis, while farmer's supplies are more plentiful in the small places. There are, though, no data on how much gossip a person is subjected to in a large city as compared to a small one. Nor are there any statistics on the amount of hospitality one meets in a large or small city or on the relative strength of kinship ties in places of various sizes. Some miscellaneous evidence has been collected in this general field, and it will be presented in order to help fill out this picture of the comparison of cities of different sizes.

DWELLINGS

One of the tasks financed recently from federal funds was the taking of inventories of real estate in various cities. As a result of these studies we have learned more about the quality of housing in the different places.[1] The cities for which studies were conducted were from 600,000 to 25,000 in population and are classified into four groups, Group 3 being cities from 600,000 to 300,000, Group 4 from 300,000 to 100,-000, Group 5 from 100,000 to 50,000, and

[1] *Real Property Inventory*, 1934, U. S. Department of Commerce, Washington.

Group 6 from 50,000 to 25,000. The samples chosen comprised about 90 per cent of the homes for each city. Only 58 cities within these population limits were studied, or about 15 for each classification.

As to the size of dwelling unit occupied by a family, the metropolis has a slightly larger proportion of small homes. The cities over 100,000 have 19 or 20 per cent of their homes with no more than three rooms, while for the cities below 100,000 the per cent is 24 or 25. These statistics are in conformity with the general opinion and with our knowledge about the size of the family in different places. About one-fifth of the dwelling units then have less than four rooms.

The per cent of overcrowded homes as judged by the investigators is almost the same as the per cent having from one to three rooms, that is, about one-fifth, except in the cities over 300,000, where the per cent of overcrowded homes is 12. That the largest cities should be judged to have less adequate space in the homes for the persons living in them is contrary to popular opinion. Since the coming of the automobile a good many families with children have moved outside the city limits where there is more space.

The newer buildings are more numerous in the larger cities. The age of buildings is of some social importance, for it is only the newest buildings that have the latest inventions in home construction, as regards heating, lighting, baths, closets, etc. It has been estimated that at the rate of building at present, a house would have to last about 150 years before being replaced. However, about 6 out of 10 houses in these cities

[22]

have been built within the last 25 years. In the cities over 300,000, 61 per cent have been built since 1909, while in the other classes of cities 56 per cent have been built since that year.

Houses not only cost more than automobiles, but they last longer. An automobile built in 1900 is quite different from one built in 1935. So is a house, but the difference is not so great. If houses wore out as fast as automobiles a larger number of houses would have more modern improvements. A house without an indoor water closet is like an ancient model of a car. Yet almost one-fifth of the houses surveyed in this investigation in 1934 in these so-called modern cities were without indoor water closets. Only 1 in 8 were without indoor toilets in the cities over 300,000, but 1 in 4 or 5 were without such facilities in the cities of fewer inhabitants. A slightly larger per cent of dwellings were without bathrooms, the percentages being 14, 21, 28, and 27, respectively, for the different sized groups,

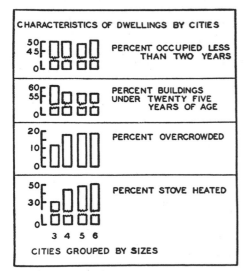

beginning with the largest. The percentages without running hot and cold water were slightly higher still: 17, 34, 38, and 36. In the cities around 100,000 in population over 1 in 3 homes were without running hot water. One other observation on these old types of dwellings concerns the nature of the

heating apparatus. Nearly 50 per cent of the houses in most of the cities are heated by stoves placed in rooms and halls, while nearly a third are heated in this manner in the very large cities with more than 300,000 inhabitants. The percentages are, respectively, 30, 45, 49, and 51.

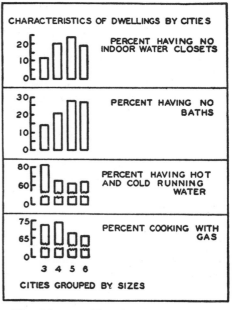

The old types of housing that survive from earlier days when living standards were lower are then represented by the houses with no inside toilets, without baths, and without running hot water. In these cities about 1 in 4 homes are of this antiquated type, and nearly 1 in 2 are without central heating and were built longer than 25 years ago. The cities with more than 300,000 inhabitants have a much smaller proportion of these old houses than do the cities around 100,000 or less inhabitants.

The existence of modern improvements can be estimated in several ways. By subtracting the various foregoing percentages from 100 the reader has an indication of the extent to which running hot water, central heating, bathing, and sanitary facilities, and other such devices have been installed. Besides these there are one or two other positive indications of modernization. Cooking with gas was an improvement that came in quite a long while ago. Still not more than two-thirds or three-quarters of the families in these cities cooked with gas. Some, of course, may have used electricity for cooking, but probably most of them cooked with coal. In the cities over 100,000 in inhabitants, 73 and 74 per cent of the families cooked with gas, while in the cities under 100,000 the percentages were 67 and 66. There are few indexes in these inventories of more advanced modernization. These investigators did collect data, however, on the extent to which mechanical refrigeration was used. Less than one-fifth of the families were supplied with electric or gas refrigerators in 1934. There has been much discussion about supplying farmers, particularly in the poorer Southeast, with electric refrigeration, since they are somewhat far removed from a daily delivery of ice. But, since in the cities less than 1 in 5 have such refrigeration, the improvement would probably spread much more slowly among the farmers, whose money incomes are much less than those of city dwellers. The use of mechanical refrigeration is growing rapidly, however.

There is one other piece of information of interest about homes, that is, the length of time a family lives in the same place. It has been observed before from records of gas meters and other similar sources that the average length of residence in one place for a family in a large city is about two years. The data from these property inventories which have supplied the figures under discussion show about the same mobility. Fifty per cent of the families had lived in their present places of abode not more than two years. But, strange to note, there was no difference between different sized cities. Mobility as so measured was no greater for cities over 100,000 than for places less than 100,000. So great a tendency to move from one habitation to another is impressive. No longer will there be for children attachment to places called home, with their families moving every two years. When such families move to different neighborhoods, the children, as well as the elders, will have to form new group connections, a process not wholly unlike uprooting a plant. The other side of the picture is that about 1 in 5 have lived in the same place for 10 years or more. The percentages are 24, 23, 24, 23; again no difference between cities of different sizes. It may be noted as an aside observation that while the median length of residence in one place is two years, the average (that is, the

TABLE I

COMPARATIVE EXPENDITURES IN CITIES

NUMBER OF DOLLARS PER THOUSAND DOLLARS SPENT IN VARIOUS TYPES OF STORES

Type of Store	POPULATION OF CITIES				
	1,000,000 and over	600,000 to 1,000,000	300,000 to 600,000	100,000 to 300,000	50,000 to 100,000
Delicatessen	$ 12	$ 5	$ 5	$ 2	$ 2
Bakery	11	10	9	8	7
Department	163	205	171	142	115
Variety	23	27	24	34	43
Men's Stores	32	25	26	26	26
Women's Specialty	44	31	39	35	33
Furriers	3.8	3.6	3.0	1.8	1.0
Motor Vehicles	52	63	79	91	97
Filling Stations	27	37	50	55	60
Public Garages	16	13	16	15	16
Furniture	20	26	21	29	30
Radio	6.6	3.9	5.5	4.8	5.7
Electric Goods	1.0	1.5	1.6	2.0	2.4
Hardware, Farm Tools	9	11	9	11	12
Coal, Wood, Ice	28	24	29	26	26
Florists	3.9	3.8	3.8	3.1	3.0
Jewelry	9.1	11.5	8.0	9.3	8.3
News Dealers	3.2	2.7	2.0	1.9	1.7
Office Equipment	6.5	7.2	8.9	9.2	5.6
Second-Hand	4.7	5.2	6.3	6.8	5.7

arithmetic mean) is somewhat longer for these cities. About half the homes are mortgaged; and as would be expected, the greater number of mortgaged homes are to be found in the larger cities, where there are more apartment houses. The percentages of mortgaged residences are 57, 56, 46, and 41 for the different classes of cities.

TRADING

Purchasers buy such goods as gasoline and groceries at the nearest place, but they go into larger cities to buy other things, such as women's hats or dress suits for men. It is not possible to secure data readily on detailed items of expenditure such as pianos or vacuum cleaners, nor is it possible to show expenditures by certain classes of purchases, but the statistics of purchases at different types of stores can be shown, as recorded in 1933 in the United States Census of Retail Distribution.

In cities of over a million inhabitants, 27 cents out of every dollar spent was spent in a food store, which is the same as the amount for smaller cities having from 10,000 to 25,000 inhabitants. Larger portions of the dollar in cities of over a million were spent in general merchandise stores, in apparel stores, and in restaurants. Less was spent in stores dealing in farmers' supplies, in automobile sales places, and with special dealers in lumber and building supplies. In the metropolis a considerably larger portion of the trader's dollar was spent in miscellaneous stores, such as beauty parlors, cigar stores, and art shops, indicating a greater differentiation and specialization of distribution. There was no difference in the portion of a dollar spent in drug stores and in furniture stores. This information is shown in percentages of the dollar in the accompanying graph.

With regard to detailed expenditures, there is more specialization in the larger cities. Thus $11 out of every $1,000 was expended in bakery stores in cities in the million population class, while only $7 was so spent in cities between 50,000 and 100,000 inhabitants. This fact probably means that there were relatively more bakeries or larger ones in the big cities than in the small places. The

fact that in delicatessen stores $12 was spent in the big cities of over 1,000,000 inhabitants, while only $2 was spent in these stores in the small cities of 50,000 to 100,000 inhabitants, is perhaps indicative of some difference in method of life for part of the

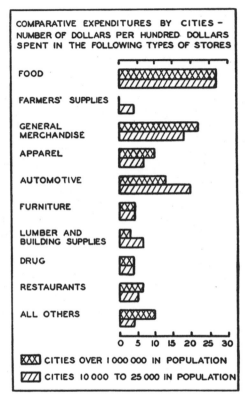

COMPARATIVE EXPENDITURES BY CITIES — NUMBER OF DOLLARS PER HUNDRED DOLLARS SPENT IN THE FOLLOWING TYPES OF STORES

FOOD
FARMERS' SUPPLIES
GENERAL MERCHANDISE
APPAREL
AUTOMOTIVE
FURNITURE
LUMBER AND BUILDING SUPPLIES
DRUG
RESTAURANTS
ALL OTHERS

0   5   10   15   20   25   30

XXX CITIES OVER 1 000 000 IN POPULATION
/// CITIES 10 000 TO 25 000 IN POPULATION

population. Expenditures in department stores are greater in the metropolis, $163, and less in the small cities, $115. But more is spent in the variety stores in the small places. In men's stores and with custom tailors $32 was spent in the large places as compared with $26 in the small places. The same difference approximately holds true for women's specialty and millinery stores. With furriers' stores, four times as much is spent in the very large cities.

The trend is the other way with motor vehicles. The figures for dealers in automobiles are $52 and $97 respectively for the large and small cities. In filling stations twice as much is spent out of the dollar in the small cities. Public vehicles are used more often in the larger cities. More money goes for hardware and farm implements in the smaller cities: $9 and $12, respectively, out of $1000 expenditure. And, curiously, more is also spent for electric goods at stores specializing in these articles in the small places, the figures being $1 and $2.50. Also, less money out of the dollar is spent in second-hand stores in the great cities.

There are certain other types of stores in which it seems quite clear that a larger portion of the annual disbursements is spent in the metropolis as compared with the small city between 50,000 and 100,000 inhabitants, as, for instance, stores selling office equipment, jewelry stores, and florist shops. Finally, about twice as large a portion of the dollar is spent with news dealers in the large cities as in the smaller ones.

The foregoing paragraphs present only a minor fragment of the shopping activities of the two types of cities. Furthermore the data do not carry us into the region of the villages, where the retail stores are quite limited in range. But it is clear that the great city offers more opportunity for trading, except possibly in farmers' supplies, hardware, and certain other such items, some of which have been indicated in previous paragraphs.

LEISURE

How leisure time is spent has been recorded in an occasional survey of a particular city or of families grouped by income classes, but these studies have not covered enough cities to make valid statistical comparisons. Only fragments of data are available.

Commercialized recreation is probably more often found in the largest cities. Such is the case with professional baseball organized into leagues. Every city above 300,000 in population has a league team, while of the cities between 100,000 and 300,000 inhabitants only 45 per cent have league baseball. Of the next class of cities in the sample, namely, those between 50,000 and 100,000, 40 per cent have organized baseball, only 15 per cent of the cities between 25,000 and 50,000 are represented in baseball leagues,

and only 10 per cent of the cities from 10,000 to 25,000 are in leagues. Few smaller places have organized ball; only one city in 60 was found in the sample.

The same thing holds true for the important professional football and hockey teams. With the one exception of the Green Bay Packers football team in Green Bay, Wisconsin, a city of 37,000 population, all of these league teams are located in cities of over 600,000 population.

Another type of leisure-time activity is represented by the Young Men's Christian Association, which is found in greater proportion in the smaller cities. The number of members per 1,000 males over 12 years of age for the different classes of cities, beginning with the largest and ending with those from 10,000 to 25,000, are 19, 43, 38, 60, 45, 52, and 67. The smaller number in the very large cities may not indicate a smaller development of this type of organized activity but rather that the Catholic and Jewish organizations have not been included in these statistics.

Time spent in hospitals is not usually considered a leisure-time activity, but the data have social significance. The statistics available are for public hospitals, the special hospitals such as those for the insane being excluded. The cities over 100,000 and under 1,000,000 have more beds per 1,000 persons, as the following numbers of beds show: 6, 10, 9, 8, 7, 7, and 7, and 6 for the places of 2,500 to 10,000.

The larger the city, the greater the opportunities of hearing symphony orchestras and operas, though this may not be as significant a datum as it was before the coming of the radio and the sound film. Thus in cities with over a million inhabitants there are on the average 4 or 5 symphony orchestras per city, while for cities between 600,000 and 1,000,-000 inhabitants there are two per city. For the other classes of cities, including all in the United States, the numbers of such symphony orchestras per 100 cities are 130, 51, 8, and 3, the last being for towns between 10,000 and 25,000 in size. The number diminishes very rapidly as the smaller cities are approached. The orchestras include civic and semi-professional symphony orchestras.

The situation is much the same with the professional opera companies, except that there are not nearly as many opera companies as there are symphony orchestras. The numbers per 100 cities of the United States by classes are 520, 133, 87, 12, and 1. Thus only one city between 25,000 and 100,000 population has an opera company, and none below 25,000.

To see museums one must visit large cities. The public museums here discussed include those dealing with art, science, history, and industry and the general museums; and of these types the first two are usually the larger. Of the cities of over one million, museums are found at the rate of 52 for each 10 cities. In cities from 500,000 to 1,000,000 the number is 23, and only 7 for cities of 250,000 to 500,000. In cities from 100,000 to 250,000 there are not quite 2 such museums for 10 cities. In the small cities, museums are very rare, there being only 1 or 2 per 100 such cities. In the towns from 2,500 to 25,000 persons there are only 7 museums per 10,000 such towns. These data are for all cities of this population range.

The information presented here should be viewed by the reader as a sample of a variety of activities. As he recalls what he has just read, the larger cities will be seen to present in general more opportunities than the smaller places. There are exceptions, but for many of the leisure-time activities the large city is the land of opportunity. This is true for modernized housing, for opportunities to trade in a great variety of lines, and for many cultural and artistic institutions. While such facts are generally known, the foregoing statistics show the degrees of difference for cities of different sizes.

CHAPTER VI

REGIONAL DIFFERENCES

Some of the differences between regions are difficult to explain, and surprisingly enough, new inventions such as the radio tend to develop new inequalities, as revealed by a comparison of cities in three different regions.

IN AN age of mobility we are not only confronted with the question of whether we had rather live in a large city or a small one, but also whether we had rather live in the western, southern, or eastern part of the United States. Comparisons by regions also face industry in seeking locations. Traders, advertisers, travelers are all concerned with such comparisons. Some differences between the regions are well known, but while there is a good deal of general information about these differences, still it is important to have extended the range of information, as, for instance, that taxation is low in the cities of the South. All cities are alike in some respects, and rural differences measure some regional characteristics better than do cities. It is also possible that as time goes on the regions may be becoming more alike, though any new invention, as for instance, the radio, will be adopted faster in one region than another. Hence inventions tend to develop new inequalities.

METHOD OF COMPARISON

Before proceeding to make the comparisons, it is necessary to make a few introductory remarks regarding the method. The United States was divided into five regions,[1] as shown in the accompanying map—the northeastern states, the southern, the middle

western, the mountain, and the Pacific Coast. In comparing cities by regions it is necessary to compare cities of approximately the same size since it has been shown that characteristics vary by size of city. A very common error, for instance, in comparing the North and the South, say, in the cost of living, is to compare the small southern town from which the migrants come, with a large eastern city to which they go, which is unfair since it costs more to live in a big city. So only cities of defined population classes were compared, for instance, cities of 50,000 to 100,000 in one region with cities of the same size in another region. In some of the population classes there were too few cities to make reliable comparisons.[2] Indeed, for most comparisons the cities of the Pacific Coast and those of the Rocky Mountain states had to be omitted, because of their small number, so that the report concerns mainly only three regions — the Northeast, the South, and the Middle West.

To determine how the cities of one region compare with another, an example will show the method. The region ranked 1 in the illustration has the most men in ratio to women, and the region ranked 3 has the fewest. The ranking of the regions for the dif-

---

[1] This division was made prior to the excellent study of regions made by Howard W. Odum, *Southern Regions of the United States* (University of North Carolina Press, 1936) in which he differentiates the Southeast from the Southwest. However, the classification here used does not differ greatly from Odum's. For the purpose of this chapter it was desirable to make the regions as large as possible to obtain enough cities.

[2] The numbers of cities of different sizes in each region are as follows:

REGION	POPULATION GROUP				
	100,000-300,000	50,000-100,000	25,000-50,000	10,000-25,000	2,500-10,000
Northeast	19	23	13	10	12
South	17	22	16	16	12
Middle West	16	20	26	17	14
Mountain	2	1	7	12	12
Pacific	3	3	7	10	10

ferent cities classified by population is:

REGION	100,000-300,000	50,000-100,000	25,000-50,000	10,000-25,000	2,500-10,000
Northeast	2	2	1½	2	3
South	3	3	3	3	2
Middle West..	1	1	1½	1	1

Clearly the cities of the Middle West have the most men and the cities of the South the fewest. In cases where the rankings are not so consistent, the actual numbers, not the rankings, are averaged for all the cities, irrespective of size, for each region. Where the difference between the averages for any two regions is not significant, no conclusion is drawn.

CHARACTERISTICS OF SOUTHERN CITIES

In population characteristics the cities of the South have the lowest percentage of immigrants of any of the regions, as is generally known. There is also the lowest percentage of men—probably because the South is a region of emigration, since men migrate in larger numbers than women. The death rate is higher, and so is the birth rate, but only slightly higher in these southern cities. Wages, both in manufacturing establishments and in retail stores, are the lowest of the three regions, but so is the monthly rent. The percentage of the adult population paying an income tax is low also. Practically all of these indices quoted mean less satisfactory economic conditions for the average inhabitant, as is also shown by the smallest percentage of radio owners.

In occupation, the South has the smallest per cent of its working population in manufacturing industries and the largest percentage engaged in trade and transportation. This fact does not mean that other regions may not have more transportation and trade, but rather that the proportion of their population engaged in these occupations is smaller than is the similar proportion in the South. Southern cities have also the smallest proportion of their working population engaged in the higher services known as the professions. This small proportion is probably due to low incomes and to fewer school teachers, who comprise a large part of the professions, for in both law and medicine the southern cities have the largest percentages

as compared with the other regions. Also the clergymen as a class constitute a larger per cent of the southern population than they do in other regions.

In regard to family life the records for cities do not bring out many outstanding characteristics for the cities of this region. There is a large percentage of widowed in the South, which may be due in part to the presence of the Negro, among whom widowhood is known to be common. The racial influence probably also accounts for the very large percentage of women employed, the large number of domestic servants, and perhaps the lowest percentage of home owners. It is not clear why the southern cities should have the largest percentages of families with lodgers nor the largest proportion of hotel keepers among their working population.

In the matter of cost of government, southern cities rank low. This means low taxes, but also less governmental expenditure for health, for public recreation, for libraries, and for schools. The number of social workers is also low. On the other hand the debt of southern cities is high.

In conclusion, it may be said by way of interpretation that the presence of Negroes, with a racial history of slavery, enters into all these calculations since they are a part of the population. Low incomes are also a basis for many of these distinguishing traits.

CITIES OF THE NORTHEAST

The outstanding population characteristic of the cities of the Northeast is the large percentage of the foreign born, due in part to proximity to the gateway to Europe. In regard to age, the ratio of young persons to the middle-aged is somewhat large as compared with the other regions, perhaps because of the presence of immigrants with the Roman Catholic religion. The proportion of elders in the eastern cities is large, doubtless attributable to the influence of New England and the migration of the younger adults westward. In these cities is found the largest percentage paying income taxes and also the highest average value of owned homes.

Among the occupations, these cities have a large percentage of their working population in manufacturing and a low percentage in trade and transportation. The percentage in personal and domestic service is low also. It is surprising to find in these cities of the Northeast the low percentages of lawyers, musicians, writers, and actors. The proportion of the clergy is small, but the church membership is highest. The high church membership may be due to the large numbers of Roman Catholics that report children as church members without their having had to make specific confession of faith, as is the case in most Protestant churches.

In the northeastern cities are found the fewest small families, the most large families, and the fewest families with lodgers. Here there are the largest numbers of single men and single women and also the smallest percentages of the population married. The sales in restaurants are low.

Government costs the most in these cities of the Northeast, more is spent for health, charities, and correction; and these cities have the largest number of police per unit of population. The large expenditures by government are accompanied by high taxes.

In concluding the presentation of data for cities of the Northeast, many of the distinguishing characteristics are accounted for in part by manufacturing, the wealth that goes with it, and by the presence of immigrants with their religion.

CITIES OF THE MIDDLE WEST

The traits of the middle western cities lie in the middle, between those of the South and those of the Northeast in many cases. Hence in only a few cases do they rank highest or lowest. In general the middle western cities are closer to those of the Northeast than to those of the South.

The cities of the Middle West have higher wages than do cities of the Northeast and, of course, than of the South. Western cities, being new, may have developed a practice of higher wages. The middle western cities also have the largest number of home owners. The cities are more recent in origin and perhaps more rapidly growing, in which case home ownership is associated with the expected financial reward of the unearned increment from increasing land values. Not only are the wages highest, but more members of the family earn a money income than is the case in the other two regions. This employment, however, is not based on the employment of children, since the cities of the Middle West have the lowest amount of

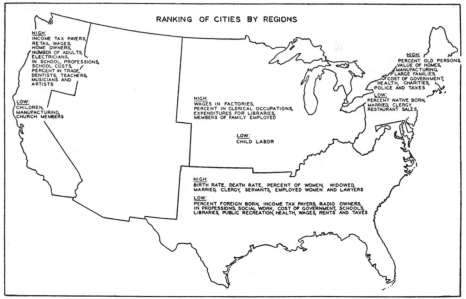

child labor. Correlated with the scarcity of child labor is the largest percentage of children in school. These middle western cities spend slightly more also on their libraries. In the occupations there are few marked distinctions. The percentage of the working population engaged in the clerical occupations and in the professions is high. So also is the percentage in industry. The proportion in architecture is high. There seems to be also a slightly larger proportion engaged as musicians, partly a function of the school system, though the tradition of music is quite strong in some of these cities, particularly where the German element is large.

CITIES OF THE PACIFIC COAST

The number of cities in the states of the Pacific Coast is small compared to the numbers in the other sections, hence it did not seem desirable to include these Pacific cities in the detailed comparisons by classes with the more numerous cities of the other regions. However, the Pacific Coast is far away from the other regions, and it comes to possess a number of distinct characteristics.

Quite distinct is the small number of children, which affects the size of family, schools, income, and many other activities of life. There is consequently a large proportion of adults, which means more of the ages that earn an income. Sales in restaurants are large on the Pacific Coast, and the number of electricians is greater than in the cities of other regions, all perhaps features of the excess of adults. Curiously, the proportion of elders is great, though no greater than in the Northeast, yet notable in a region in which there is a large proportion of immigrants. Generally the old people are not ready immigrants. Wages are high in the Pacific region, as are the proportion paying income taxes and the number having radios.

As to occupational activities the cities of the Pacific Coast are in the main trading centers with, however, a quite large sprinkling of the professions, especially teachers, musicians, writers, and artists. Church membership is low. Many who migrate do not transfer their church membership. The support of schools and libraries is liberal.

It may be observed that most of these characteristics in which the Pacific Coast cities outrank those of the other regions flow from the large percentage of adults and amount of wealth.

CHAPTER VII

URBAN RESEMBLANCES AND REGIONAL DIFFERENCES

Regional comparisons so common in the past have been upset to a degree by the appearance of cities, which have many resemblances.

CITIES differ by regions, and so do non-urban regions. A southern planter differs from a New England farmer as truly as a Charlestonian differs from a Bostonian. Indeed, there is reason to think that the farm and village areas differ from one region to another more widely than do cities. Visitors to any country — China, Russia, India, or France — are sometimes advised to see the villages and rural peoples on the theory that the habits and manners of city people everywhere are much more alike than are those of rural areas. Whether or not this is true is a question.

THEORY THAT CITIES ARE MORE ALIKE THAN RURAL REGIONS

This theory is based upon the thought that the agencies of communication, such as the railroad, make resemblances between one city and another by dissemination of common traits such as the magazines or the same brands of clothing. Cities are creatures of transportation and are hence on the highways of contact, so that any new cultural element tends in general to spread to all the cities more easily than it would spread to the rural areas, which are somewhat off the beaten highway. In general an isolated island or mountainous tract is more likely to develop and maintain local peculiarities than places on the trade routes. Thus dialects were at one time many and could be found in localities cut off somewhat by barriers of mountain, water, or desert. But travel and communication tend to break down such dialects and other peculiarities of custom. So the city streets in Atlanta, Seattle, and Jersey City are much alike, with the same type of shops, electric signs, and advertisements of cigarettes, whereas in rural regions the local differentiations of a century ago may persist. Such at least is the theory. What do the facts show?

EVIDENCE ON GREATER RESEMBLANCE OF CITIES

In order to test out this theory, 18 social characteristics were chosen for noting whether they were more nearly the same in cities or whether the rural regions resembled one another more closely in the degree that these characteristics were possessed by them. These traits are the following: Ratio of the young to the middle-aged, ratio of the old to the middle-aged, size of family, percentage of adults married, percentage widowed, percentage of children in school, sex ratio of the single, amount of rent, home ownership, percentage paying income taxes, birth rate, death rate, percentage of foreign-born, automobiles per capita, telephones, radio, postal receipts, and church membership. These 18 characteristics were chosen quite at random in so far as any idea of using them in comparing resemblances of cities and of rural districts was concerned. They were chosen because the data had already been collected.

The use made of the traits may be illustrated by a consideration of the first listed, namely the number of youth. The idea was to find out whether the cities differed from one another more in the percentage of youth in the population than did the rural districts. In the southern states, including Texas, Oklahoma, and Arkansas, in 17 cities between 100,000—300,000 population, the number of the young was 63 per cent of the number of adults. In 19 cities of the same population class in the Northeast, including New England and the North Atlantic States, the per cent was 69. The difference between the cities of the Northeast and the cities of the South is only 6, not much difference for the regions by cities. On the other hand, for 43 rural counties (with no city over 2,500 in a county) in the South and 42 rural counties in the Northeast the difference was 20, as compared with 6, the difference between the cities. In other words, the difference between the average percentage of youths in the cities of the two regions is much less than the average difference in this respect between the county districts of these regions. The cities resemble one another between the North and the South more than do the rural regions in this particular characteristic of young people. The conclusion with respect to this trait, then, supports the theory stated at the beginning of the discussion.

The cities have fewer young than do the rural regions. This fact is probably occasioned by migration of older persons to cities and by birth control in cities; both factors are probably the result of the transportation and communication inventions. Why there should be such a difference between the rural counties of the North and the South is not known, but perhaps birth control has spread little to the rural counties of the South and more to those of the North. In support of this explanation the difference between the average birth rates of the cities of the Northeast and South and of the rural counties of the two regions shows that the cities are more alike in the birth rate than are the rural districts.

But to return to the young in city and country, the same greater resemblance of cities than of rural counties is shown when the South is compared with the Middle West, which is here defined as including the Dakotas on the west and Ohio on the east. On the contrary when the northeastern states are compared with the middle western states the rural counties resemble one another more than do the cities. Why this is so is not known. Grain farming is common to the rural counties of these regions in large part, and the time of settlement was not so greatly separated, nor so early, as on the Atlantic seaboard. Thus in the case of the number of young people the cities of differ-

ent regions resembled each other more than did the rural counties in two out of three regional comparisons.

A characteristic in which the rural counties are rather uniform and in which the cities are varied is the presence of a foreign-born population. Country districts have few foreign-born, while the cities have more; but the rural counties are alike in having few, while some cities have a great many and others only a few. Hence in regard to this trait the farms and villages are alike, while the cities differ.

Of these eighteen characteristics previously listed the cities of the Northeast and the South were more alike than were the rural counties of the two regions in 11 out of 18 traits, while the rural counties resembled one another more than did the cities in 7 out of the 18. The cities tended, then, to resemble each other somewhat more than did the rural regions. When the South was compared with the Middle West in 10 of the traits the cities were more alike, and in 8 the rural counties were more uniform. The situation was reversed when the Northeast and Middle West were compared, the rural counties being more uniform in 11 cases and the cities in only 7. The theory that cities are more alike from one region to. another than are the rural districts depends, then, on the regions being compared and on the traits considered. This evidence regarding traits chosen at random without regard to the theory does not give conclusive support to the theory that cities of different regions are more alike than the rural regions.

With regard to the traits used in the comparisons, cities tend to be more alike in regard to the following traits: size of family, home ownership, the percentage of youth, the percentage of old people, the sex ratio of the single, the birth rate, ownership of automobiles, telephones, and radios. The rural counties on the other hand resemble one another more in the rent paid; the percentage married, widowed, paying income taxes, and foreign-born; death rates; and church membership.

THE THEORY OF SPECIALIZED CITIES

A little reflection on the foregoing resem-

blances and differences indicates that perhaps the greater number of contacts of cities
with one another could probably account
for a few of the traits in which they tend to
be alike. A perusal of those traits in which
cities differ more than do rural counties, such
as, for instance, the foreign-born, suggests
that there may be specialized cities. Communication and transportation instead of
making all cities alike may lead to division
of labor and specialization between them—a
second theory. With regard to this theory
that cities specialize and hence become different, it would seem that this is more likely
to occur among smaller cities than large
ones, as large cities are a collection of different trades and industries. For instance,
among these large cities (100,000—300,000
in population) in the three regions, there
were 28 resemblances; while for a group of
smaller cities (50,000—100,000) there were
only 24 resemblances, thus suggesting that
large cities may specialize less than smaller
ones.

THE THEORY THAT A CITY OF ONE REGION RESEMBLES A CITY OF ANOTHER REGION MORE THAN IT DOES THE RURAL DISTRICTS OF ITS OWN REGION

There is another phase of this subject.
Does an urban Yankee differ from a southern
city dweller more than he differs from one of
his own rural neighbors? Perhaps so at the
time of the Civil War, but now Boston may
be more like Atlanta than it is like rural
Dukes County in Massachusetts. Let us see
how such a question is answered with regard
to home ownership. Cities have less home
ownership than do villages and farm areas
generally. In this particular the southern
cities are more like northeastern cities than
they are like southern rural counties. Also,
the cities of the Northeast are more like
southern cities in extent of home ownership
than they are like neighboring rural counties.
In other words, the differences are greater
within the regions than they are between the
cities of the two regions. For these two
regions, regional differences are not so great
as urban rural differences. In 14 out of 18
characteristics the cities of the South and
North are more alike than southern cities

are like southern rural counties.

The situation is different in regard to the
possession of the radio, for the similarities
within the southern region and within the
northeastern region are greater than the similarities between the cities in the two regions.
This observation seems strange in the case
of the radio. It is generally known that the
number of radios per 1,000 population is
greater in cities than in rural regions. Yet
in 1930 the farmer-villager and the city man
were more alike in the South in not possessing a radio than the urban dwellers of the
South and Northeast were in possessing one.
The low income of the South has probably
acted as a barrier to diffusion in cities as
truly as it has in the poorer rural counties.[1]

In a few traits other than the possession
of radios there was more rural-urban resemblance within a region than interregional
urban resemblance. Such was the case in
regard to the possession of motor cars, in the
per cent married, and in the number of
foreign-born. In these four cases resemblances within the regions are greater than
between regions.

But in most other traits, the cities of two
regions were more alike than were the cities
and the rural counties. This was the case
for size of family, average rent, per cent paying income taxes, number of young people,
number of old people, sex ratio of the unmarried, birth rates, death rates, home
ownership, telephones, postal receipts, and
church membership. In these traits urban
interregionalism was less than urban-rural
intraregionalism. There were exceptions, of
course, in some of the comparisons, but the

---

[1] In this comparison the average radio per capita was compared by region and by urban and
rural communities. The differences are differences between the averages. This may not be the
best technique. Another way is to measure, let us
say, the scatter or range of the different cities of
a region in the possession of a radio as shown by
the average deviation of the cities from the average city. Thus if the cities of the North and
South are thrown together their average deviation
in per capita radios may be compared with the
average deviation when the cities and the rural
counties are thrown together. When measured in
this manner, the conclusion is not changed from
that reached when the differences between averages were compared. This second technique was
used to check conclusions found by the first
method.

foregoing summary is based upon a clear majority of the various comparisons for a particular trait.

IMPLICATIONS OF THE CONCLUSION THAT URBAN-RURAL DIFFERENCES ARE GREATER THAN REGIONAL URBAN DIFFERENCES

There are several possible implications of the fact that in many traits cities of different regions resemble each other more than they do the surrounding hinterland. One is that it is probably not wise to make regional comparisons in regard to those traits, such as sex ratios, number of old people, etc., in which the cities of different regions are so much alike. At least when such comparisons are made the cities should be excepted. There is a good deal of loose, exaggerated talk about regional differences, whereas actually the cities of the different regions have many resemblances. At least it should be borne in mind that urban-rural differences very often overshadow regional differences.

Another implication concerns the nature of representation in legislative assemblies, which is on a geographical if not a regional basis. A representative to Congress from San Francisco and one from New York may have nearer the same constituents in many traits than one or the other would have, respectively, with a representative from a rural region of California or a rural region of New York State. There is probably little to be done practically about changing the nature of representation, but a recognition of these resemblances and differences is important in interpreting representation.

Above all, however, the data show that regional comparisons so common in the past have been upset to a degree by the appearance of cities, which cut across regional lines.

CHAPTER VIII

THE AVERAGE CITY

*Here is presented "Averagetown," the typical American city.
What do the people do, who are they, how much do they earn,
what is the family like, and how much tax does the citizen pay?*

WE OFTEN speak of the average man. So also we may hear a person refer to a place as just an average town. Occasionally novelists have written stories about an average city. No doubt politicians have it in mind when they are sizing up public opinion. Traveling salesmen have their own ideas of what the average city is like. Historians would also like very much to have had an accurate description of the average town in the times of the Roman Empire, or in England in the Middle Ages. Visitors to other countries have something of the same query. The average town in the United States was different before the Civil War from what it is now and from what it will be in the future.

There is therefore some interest in trying to record the characteristics of the average American city in 1930. The traits presented will all be those statistically measurable. They may not be as interesting as those a tourist might observe, but they will probably be more accurately described. Still it is interesting to know how much rent the average family pays in the average city. It is also worth while knowing how much debt the average city carries, or what the tax is per capita. It is also important to know the occupations followed by the inhabitants of the average city, how many have radios, and what proportion are unmarried. Once such measurements are known they may become a standard with which to compare our own city. We may then know how much and in what respects our home town differs from the average town and in this way come to know the distinguishing features of the city in which we live.

How the Average City Was Found

The first problem is to determine what is the average city. Since the idea of the average town is the keynote to the descriptions which follow, it is highly desirable to be sure to pick the average city. Therefore it is necessary to go in some detail into the method by which this was done. There are various ways of determining an average city. In the first place one might guess that the average city has around 50,000 inhabitants or less. Since 1790 the United States Census has published the population of places of over 8,000 inhabitants, usually considered as cities. In 1930 the average population of such cities was 49,900. If villages under 8,000 had been included, the population of the average place would have been lower. Or it would be possible to determine average characteristics of the total urban territory in the United States, ranging from villages of 2,500 to New York City. Such an average would tend to be rather abstract because such a variety of sizes of places would be included.

These extremes could be avoided by choosing a sample of cities that have around 50,000 inhabitants. But what towns to choose? It would seem desirable to omit such specialized towns as, say, Atlantic City, New Jersey, or Gary, Indiana, since they seem to be quite different from the typical. Such divergences as are found in these two cities are usually noted in the occupations, espe-

[36]

cially in manufacturing, trade, and transportation. For the total urban area it is easily ascertained that 38 per cent of the working population are in manufacturing, 16 per cent in trade, and 10 per cent in transportation. Gary, Indiana, has 59 per cent in manufacturing while Atlantic City has only 19 per cent, as contrasted with the average of 38 per cent. In the latter city those in domestic and personal service outnumber those in manufacturing 2 to 1, while in Gary they are only one-seventh. So occupations of the population are often a key to the peculiarities of a city.

Accordingly a group of cities between 25,000 and 100,000 in population were chosen from which to compute the characteristics of the average city. The working populations of these cities chosen for study were engaged in transportation to the extent of about 10 per cent, in trade to about 16 per cent, while 38 per cent were in manufacturing, which per cents are the averages for the total urban areas. Data on 33 such cities distributed proportionately in all parts of the United States except the South were recorded, and the averages of these data were considered to be the characteristics of the average city. The average city here described is not, then, a single city but a composite of cities much alike in size and occupations. It is probably, though, much like a single typical city. It was decided to omit from the calculations the cities from the southern states because of the presence of such large numbers of Negroes and so many domestic and personal servants. However, the data on 18 such southern cities were used in determining the characteristics of the average southern city in the United States. Such, then, is the way in which the average city was determined.

WHAT THE PEOPLE DO

The largest class of workers consists of those in manufacturing. A little over one-third (37 per cent) of the population at work are making things. Or to put it another way, nearly two-thirds of the people who work are not making any object which they can exchange for things to eat (which are not raised in the average city) or for other necessities which they do not produce. Between one-fifth and one-sixth (17 per cent) are buying and selling and in that way making the money with which to buy the things they need. About one-tenth are engaged in moving objects and persons from one place to another. Slightly more than one in ten (10.7 per cent) are following an occupation little developed in former times, namely, writing, copying, figuring, filing, etc. The inhabitants of Averagetown require one in eight or nine persons (11.6 per cent) of the working population to render them personal services, such as preparing and serving food, laundering, cleaning, cutting hair, etc. There is a higher type of service requiring much more training, as in law, teaching, medicine, dentistry, and other professions. About one in 11 (8.7 per cent) is required for such high grade services. Finally, one in 50 is normally engaged in some public service, such as protecting property from fire and theft, inspecting, and in doing various services for the city.

The average city requires about three (2.7) police for every one-thousand of the ordinarily employed population. A slightly larger number (3.7) of officials and inspectors and guards are needed. To minister to our physical ills four (3.9) physicians are available for every one thousand of the working population. The need for a lawyer seems to be slightly greater (4.2) and that of a preacher slightly less (3.1). All these services appear to be necessities. On the other hand, music, which may not be considered so much a necessity, calls for more teachers and performers (4.8) than there are doctors, preachers, or lawyers. About six times as many teachers (23.8) as there are in any one of these other professions are wanted by the inhabitants.

There is not much difference in the occupations attracting the people in the average southern city from those in the average city for the rest of the nation (which is sometimes referred to as the northern city, although the sample is balanced as to far West, Middle West, and New England). The average town of the South has more lawyers, preachers, and doctors per 1,000 ordinarily employed but fewer teachers. The most striking difference is in the greater number of servants; there are about twice as many per 100 workers in the southern city as in the northern. A much smaller proportion are in manufacture, 27 per cent as compared with 37 per cent in the North.

WHO THE CITIZENS ARE

In the average city 2 out of 3 persons are of native white stock, born of native-born parents. This proportion is about the same in the northern and southern city. But in the southern city one person out of 3 that one meets is likely to be a Negro; while in the northern city he will be either foreign-born or the son or daughter of an immigrant. Of those who are not of native stock one out of 3 will be foreign born and the other 2 will be children of foreign-born parents.

Most of the citizens of the average city are old enough to hold down a job but not so old as to be shelved, that is, they are between 20 and 55 years old. The number of those under 20 years of age is about two-thirds the number of adults of working age. Assuming that those under 20 years of age should still be in school or are out of a job, then there is a burden of two young people for every three of working age. Actually the burden is probably not quite so large, since a good many young persons between, say, 18 and 20 are at work. Those over 55 years of age we have defined as old, though some over this age may resent the adjective. The age at which industry lays a man off the job or refuses to rehire him is a variable. But if 55 is an average retirement age, then every 3 or 4 of the working population of working age would have one elder to support, assuming the old people have not saved enough money to support themselves. But whatever the ratio may be of those who do not pay their way to those who do, the average city has 62 per cent as many young as it has people of working age and 28 per cent as many old. The city has a population largely of middle-aged persons.

The average city is slightly more attractive to women than to men, if we take their presence to be an indication, for there are only 97 men to every 100 women in the average city.

WHO WORKS — HIS EARNINGS

While there are more women in the average city than there are men, those who earn a money income are largely the men. Yet in this generalized typical city, one in every 4 adult women is working outside the home. In the South, where there are many Negro women employed away from home, over one in 3 adult women (36 per cent) are ordinarily employed. The married woman generally is not employed for wages, and if she has been employed before her marriage she soon gives up her job. Yet in the average city one in 8 (13 per cent) married women was employed in 1930. This means that 7 in 8 were presumably supported by their husbands, to whom they no doubt rendered valuable aid as home makers. In a previous paragraph an approach was made to estimating the ratio of the young and old to the population of working age. Adjusting the estimates to the number of married women not at work, it seems probable that for every 100 persons of the working population there are 125 to 150 persons who do not earn any money and who are supported in part or in full by those who do.

How much does the average person at work earn in the typical city? It is difficult to determine precisely, but the average person employed in a factory earns at the rate of about $1,300 a year. This figure is determined by dividing the total factory pay roll of the city by the sum of the average number employed per month in factories. The rate is thus probably underestimated, but the actual earnings of an average employee are probably less, since unemployment or partial employment is not considered. This figure includes payments to women and young persons as well as to men. In retail stores the figure is about the same, $1350.

In the typical city of the South the rate of earnings is lower, $960 in manufacturing and $1,190 in retail stores. It is realized of course that any average figure of rates or actual earnings is a composite and obscures much information which a particular reader might want to know, but these figures here quoted do give a rough idea of what the average wage earner in the typical city receives a year.

WHERE THE JONESES LIVE

The average family that rents a dwelling pays $28 a month for it. This figure is undoubtedly higher than the median rent, or the rent paid by the typical wage earner. In the South the average rent is $18. This wide discrepancy may be deceptive in that there is probably not so great a difference between the rents of typical houses. Into the average of the South go large numbers of Negro houses with extremely low rentals. There is no such discrepancy in the value of the owned home, which is $5,000 in the North and $4,600 in the South, where the Negro seldom owns his home. With the status of the Negro as it is, it is not surprising then that only 35 per cent of all families own their homes in the average city of the South, while 50 per cent own them in the North. Every other family in the average city of the North had a radio in 1930, but in the South only one in every 4 or 5 families had one. About one in 40 or 50 dwellings is an apartment house, that is, a house with three or more families, and for the whole urban area one in every five families lives in such a house. For the average city the ratio might be nearer one in 10, as a guess.

WHAT THE FAMILY IS LIKE

The family in Averagetown consists generally of only 3 or 4 persons, including boarders and relatives, considering 2 persons as a minimum family. More exactly, 100 families contain in the average northern city 333 persons, which is 3.3 persons per family. In the average southern city the number is 3.5. About one in 10 families has roomers or boarders.

Concerning children, on the average each 100 women between the ages of 20 and 45 years have 38 children under five years of age; while about 2 out of 3 families (65 per cent) have no children under 10 years of age. The time required for child care diminishes rapidly after a child reaches 10 years of age. So large a percentage of families without young children helps to explain why so many wives (or other home makers) are employed outside the home: 15 per cent, or one in 6 or 7, in the average city. In fact a rather large number of families have more than one breadwinner; one in 3 families, or 31 per cent of all families, in 1930 had more than one person bringing in a money income. A young person in normal times often faces a choice as to whether to go to work or continue in school. Nearly everyone nowadays finishes the elementary school, but not all go to high school. Those who do not go to high school have the doors of many opportunities shut to them. There is some interest in knowing how many children go to high school in the average city. Much depends on the state and the state laws. But in the North two-thirds (68 per cent) of the young persons 16 and 17 years of age are in school, while in the South 54 per cent of these ages attend school.

Not everyone forms a family of course. In the average city, 6 out of every 10 adults over 15 years of age are married, and about one in 10 is widowed or divorced. Thus 3 in 10 are single, which in modern times may result from the demands of civilization being so great that not many young persons between 15 and 18 can get married. In any case 4 out of 10 persons beyond the biological age for marriage in the average city are not married, whatever may be the social significance.

CITIZEN AND HIS GOVERNMENT

A city government is a collective activity of the citizens for their own interests and welfare. Of the collective services rendered most are considered quite essential. How much do they cost in the average city? The average tax was $43 for each person over 15 years of age for the year 1930 in the average city. It was $10 lower in the average southern city. The payment of the tax may be said to come out of the pockets of those who receive money incomes, which is approximately the same group as the working population. The tax load on the average citizen who works is probably then around $80 in the average city. This is about one-seventeenth of the average wage earner's annual income; but there is not much meaning to this fraction, since taxes are distributed unequally and the incidence is not always known.

Viewed in another way, the tax is only $32 a year per capita. What does the average person get for $32? Police protecion, garbage collection, the use of paved streets, etc. Whether he could get more for that $32 if he spent it for other things is a question which each one may ask himself. But he gets a good deal for his taxes in goods and services that are essential. If the amount spent were broken down, schools would receive a large share, libraries, health, and recreation much less.

The resident of the average city has not paid as he went along. So his city is in debt. The amount in the average city is probably not excessive: $70 per capita, or probably $180 per working adult, whose average income is somewhere around $1,300. In any case his city is a useful corporation in which to invest, even if it renders services and not dividends. Careful watching of the investment would, however, increase the yield to the "stockholders"—the citizens.

CHAPTER IX

DIFFERENT TYPES OF CITIES

What are the distinguishing characteristics of trading centers, factory towns, transportation centers, mining towns, pleasure resorts, health resorts, and college towns?

SPECIALIZATION is characteristic of modern times. Cities, like men, specialize. Atlantic City is a pleasure resort; Washington a capital; Princeton, New Jersey, a college town; Rochester, Minnesota, a health center; and Gary, Indiana, a steel town. All these differ from the average city previously described. The cities that are different are perhaps more interesting than the average city.

What are the distinguishing characteristics of these cities that specialize in one type of activity? Some characteristics are obvious. Atlantic City has many hotels to accommodate the visitors who come seeking pleasure. Gary has many mill workers. Rochester has hospitals and clinics. There are other char-

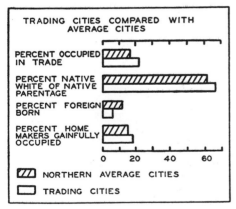

TRADING CITIES COMPARED WITH AVERAGE CITIES

PERCENT OCCUPIED IN TRADE

PERCENT NATIVE WHITE OF NATIVE PARENTAGE

PERCENT FOREIGN BORN

PERCENT HOME MAKERS GAINFULLY OCCUPIED

0   20   40   60

▨ NORTHERN AVERAGE CITIES

▢ TRADING CITIES

acteristics not so obvious. College towns, for instance, have more than the average supply of widows. Capitals have many clerical workers. The presence of such characteristics may sometimes be correctly discerned without statistics and reported vividly by

using descriptive terms carrying no measurement of degree. Visitors to any of these places, by using the license of the cartoonist to exaggerate selected traits out of all proportion, can delineate for us various characteristics. But generally traits so described do not stand out in the statistics as markedly as they do in impressionistic language. Thus Sweden is the home of the true Nordic—tall long-headed peoples with blond hair and blue eyes. Yet actual measurements show that only 15 per cent of the Swedish population actually possess this combination of traits which the traveler so readily reports.

Again most cities that specialize do not do so as wholeheartedly, so to speak, as does Hollywood. The specialization is to only a slight degree. Furthermore, as one swallow doesn't make a summer, so one city doesn't establish a type, certainly not for less obvious characteristics. In determining a type one must observe a large number of cities from different parts of the country and of different sizes in order to eliminate the characteristics peculiar to any one region or to cities of any one size. To describe accurately and reliably the various characteristics of so-called specialized cities is then not easily done. An additional limitation is that information on many different traits about which we should like to know is not collected by the Census or any other agency. However, the attempt has been made and the results follow.

TRADING CENTERS

The first class of cities to be presented is a very common one—cities which have a rather large percentage of their population engaged in trade. The average city has 17 per cent of its working population busy in buying and selling. In this study any city with more than 20 per cent in trade was chosen as a trading town. Twenty-three cities were studied and the average population was 48,500.[1]

Even in the cities having well above the average amount of trade the percentage engaged in manufacturing is greater than the percentage in trade. The per cent in trade averages 22 per cent, and is smaller than the percentage, 27, in manufacturing. Nearly all cities are considered to be either trading centers, manufacturing centers, or varying degrees of mixture of the two. However there seems to be no city which does not have a large per cent in manufacture. This may seem strange to those who identify manufacturing with large factories. But there is much fabrication of many different things done outside large factories.

These cities with a somewhat large proportion of their population engaged in trade have slightly more servants (15 per cent) and also more in the professions (9.7 per cent) than the average city. This larger percentage of professional men and women holds for physicians (.46), lawyers (.56), clergymen (.47), musicians (.57) and teachers (2.64). The annual earnings rate is lower, though, than in the average city—$1,240 in manufacturing and $1,310 in retail trade. The average house rent, $26, is a little lower, as is the average value of homes occupied by their owners, $4,560.

Trading cities have proportionately more native born whites of native parents, 67 per cent, than the average city. There are only 6 per cent foreign born in these trading cities.

In this particular sample of cities the percentage of the population over 15 years of age who were married was a little high (62 per cent) and the sex ratio of the single was

a little low (110) as compared with the average city. The low proportion of old, 25 per cent, to middle aged and the high percentage of young, 65 per cent, may be due to the fact that many of these cities were in the West and South rather than to the fact that they were trading centers.

In regard to various other attributes studied, the trading centers were not specially marked. They are then, in summary, low in rank in manufactures, high in professions, not conspicuously high in income and values of homes, rather to the contrary. There are few foreign born, a fairly large per cent married. It is not clear though that all such characteristics inevitably flow from the fact that the cities have a large percentage in trade.

FACTORY TOWNS

The *raison d'etre* of cities in general, in the past, has been that a person could make enough money to buy food by doing something else. Usually he is either trading or making some material object. These are the

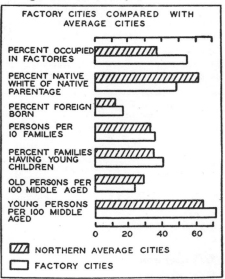

essential activities which explain why the population is there. Once there, they must have policemen, laundrymen, doctors, and others providing subsidiary services. Some cities have less trading and fewer of these other services while they have more engaged in manufacturing. Among those cities that

---

[1] Amarillo, Corpus Christi, Waco, and Wichita Falls, Texas; Bangor, Maine; Cedar Rapids and Sioux City, Iowa; Enid, Oklahoma; Fargo, North Dakota; Fort Smith and Little Rock, Arkansas; Harrisburg, Pennsylvania; Hutchinson and Wichita, Kansas; Lincoln, Nebraska; Orlando, Florida; Riverside, San Jose, Santa Ana, and Fresno, California; Sioux Falls, South Dakota; Springfield and Joplin, Missouri.

have chiefly manufacturing as an occupation, there are many different kinds. A small southern cotton mill town with many women workers is quite different in many categories from a large steel town with many male laborers. In studying cities that specialize in manufacturing, the various types have been thrown together, except in regard to size, and no attempt has been made to describe the different types of manufacturing places.

The main sample of manufacturing cities[2] for this study were between 25,000 and 100,-000 in population, the average being 49,000. They were places where 45 per cent or more of the working population were in manufacturing establishments. Each of the cities also had less than 18 per cent in trade and less than 10 per cent in transportation. The average per cent in manufacturing was 55, in trade 12, and in transportation 6 per cent. These cities were chosen outside the orbit of a metropolis. It is of some interest to see what are the social characteristics of these factory towns. Quite a small per cent were in domestic and personal service (8.8) and also in the professions (6.3). There were only about half as many lawyers as were found in the average city. Physicians, teachers, and musicians were about three-quarters as many, while the clergy were about seven-eighths as numerous as in the average city of the same size.

While the police were the same in proportion in the factory towns and in the average city, the proportion of inspectors is twice as large in the manufacturing centers. The average rental, $26, is a little lower, the average value of the owned home, $5,500, is higher than in the average city, and the percentage of those owning homes is low. School attendance is also low. There are fewer old

people, more young people, and the number of children is large. The ratio of single men to single women is high, 123, with a slight excess in the percentage, 61, married. The percentage of foreign born is high, 17. The average annual earnings ($1,260) in manufacturing are lower than in the average city.

In the larger factory towns over 100,000 in population of which there were 16 in number in the sample for this study, the proportion of children and young adults is low in contrast to the medium sized factory towns. This may be due to many of these cities being in New England where the percentage of children is small. In the smaller factory towns under 25,000 in inhabitants, 10 in number in this study, many of which are in the South, there is a very high percentage of young adults and a low sex ratio. These conditions are undoubtedly due to the presence of a large number of young girls working in the mills. The number of foreign born is also small in this sample. The statistical picture of the factory town is much as one would have expected.

TRANSPORTATION CENTERS

In the average city not quite 10 per cent of the population gainfully occupied is in transportation. With transportation activities connected with railroads, trucks, warehouses, cabs, etc. using so small a proportion of the working population, it is a question whether any characteristics of note for such cities will be shown in the statistics. The criterion of selection was that these cities did not have a large per cent in trade nor in manufacturing. They contain over 12.5 per cent in transportation and not over 38 per cent in manufacturing and not over 19 per cent in trade. For this group of cities, 26 in number,[3] the per cent in transportation was 15.7, in manufacturing, 33, and in trade, 16. The average population was 46,-

[2] Sharon, Lebanon, Bethlehem, and York, Pennsylvania; Brockton, Fitchburg, Haverhill, Lawrence, and Taunton, Massachusetts; Hamilton, Lorain, and Middletown, Ohio; Jamestown, New York; Kenosha, Racine, and Sheboygan, Wisconsin; Lewiston, Maine; Manchester and Nashua, New Hampshire; Michigan City, Muncie, Kokomo, and Anderson, Indiana; Moline and Rockford, Illinois; Muskegon and Pontiac, Michigan; Port Arthur, Texas; Durham, Winston-Salem, and High Point, North Carolina; Meriden, Bristol, Torrington, Waterbury, and New Britain, Connecticut.

[3] Altoona, Pennsylvania; Ashland, Covington, and Paducah, Kentucky; Auburn, and Elmira, New York; Clinton, Council Bluffs, and Ottumwa, Iowa; Cumberland, Maryland; Danville, East St. Louis, and Galesburg, Illinois; Galveston, Texas; Green Bay and Superior, Wisconsin; Hoboken, New Jersey; Marion, Ohio; Mobile, Alabama; Monroe, Louisiana; Ogden, Utah; Pensacola, Florida; Port Huron, Michigan; Portland, Maine; Roanoke, Virginia; Savannah, Georgia.

300. The social characteristics were much like those of the manufacturing cities.

The transportation centers were below the average number in the various professions except in the case of clergymen, but numbers of professional men and women were not

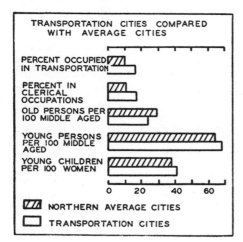

nearly so far below the average as in industrial towns. School costs, $21 per adult and $66 per student per year, and school attendance, 61 per cent of those 16 and 17 years of age, were low. Not so many owned homes, 46 per cent, as in the average city and the rents paid, $24, were lower. The percentage married was a little higher, 61, and there were more families taking in boarders and lodgers, 12 per cent. The retail wage was low, $1,260 a year. There were fewer old persons and more children and young adults. Also fewer families had radios, 41 per cent, in 1930. The percentage of foreign-born is smaller than in the industrial towns. The picture of the transportation center is then much like that of the factory town, only less extreme in differing from the average city.

MINING TOWNS

Mining towns are smaller than industrial, trade, or transportation centers, being generally under 25,000 in inhabitants. For these smaller places the United States Census does not publish as much information as for places over this size. Hence it is not possible to determine many of the characteristics. The 30 mining towns from 10,000 to 25,000 in

population averaged 15,800.[4] An outstanding characteristic is the large number of children and young people. There were 83 young persons under 20 to every 100 from 20 to 55 years of age. There were also 49 children under five years of age to every 100 women 20 to 45 years of age. These are the largest numbers of young persons found in any of the types of cities. This characteristic of a large number of children is said to be true of mining towns in the European countries also. The number of old persons over 55 years of age per 100 adults 20 to 55 years of age is very low, 12, but no lower than in the factory towns. The rent is low, $25, as is also the average value of the owned homes, $4,330. The number of owned homes is, however, near the average for the nation. Wages are low in both manufacturing, $1,190, and in retail trade, $1,230. The number of single males is high, 124 to 100 single females, and the percentage married is lower than in factory towns, 59, which is

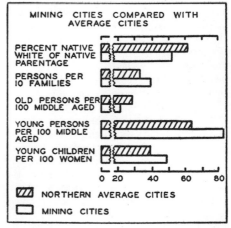

probably due to the large numbers of young persons. The percentage of foreign-born, 14, is above average but not quite as high as in the factory towns.

[4] Anaconda, Montana; Arkansas City and El Dorado, Kansas; Barre and Rutland, Vermont; Bedford, Indiana; Bellaire, Ohio; Corsicana and Tyler, Texas; Hibbing and Virginia, Minnesota; Iron Mountain, Ironwood, and Menominee, Michigan; Mt. Carmel, Oil City, Old Forge, Olyphant, Pittston, Plymouth, Carbondale, Dunmore, Mahanoy City, Shamokin, Shenandoah, Tamaqua, Kingston, and Pottsville, Pennsylvania; Ponca City, Oklahoma; West Frankfort, Illinois.

Pleasure Resorts

In a pleasure resort, not every one is engaged in having a good time. The number who go there for pleasure is often small as compared to the normal population. Such would be the case with Biloxi, Mississippi, or Newport, Rhode Island. Sometimes the pleasure features are only for a short season. The advertisement which Aiken, South Caro-

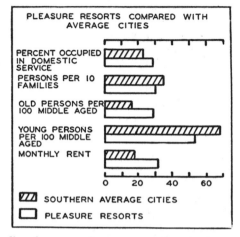

PLEASURE RESORTS COMPARED WITH AVERAGE CITIES

PERCENT OCCUPIED IN DOMESTIC SERVICE

PERSONS PER 10 FAMILIES

OLD PERSONS PER 100 MIDDLE AGED

YOUNG PERSONS PER 100 MIDDLE AGED

MONTHLY RENT

0   20   40   60

▨ SOUTHERN AVERAGE CITIES

☐ PLEASURE RESORTS

lina, has as a pleasure resort is out of proportion to the relative numbers who go there for the winter climate. Most of the pleasure resorts are small,[5] the average population of those here studied being 13,900. Hence the data for them are limited, as the Census presents few statistics for the small places.

The characteristics of the pleasure resorts are different from those of the factory and mining towns as would be expected. The average rent paid, $31, is higher than for the average city as is also the average value of homes, $6,200, although the manufacturing wage is low, $1,230. In the cities that specialize in pleasure, there is an excess of women, of widowed persons, and of the older persons. The sex ratio of the single is 99 women to 100 men, much lower than the

average. There are 32 persons over 55 years of age per 100 who are from 20 to 55 years of age, while the percentage widowed is 11, somewhat higher than the average. In general this group of widowed, old persons, and women is one that does not earn a money income. On the other hand children who are also not income producing are slightly fewer in the pleasure resorts than in the average city. Perhaps the older persons have accumulated some property and live in part on the income.

There are three cities of this pleasure-resort type that have large populations, Atlantic City, New Jersey; Miami, Florida; and St. Petersburg, Florida. For these three cities there is some additional information. In the occupations in these cities is found a very large proportion engaged in domestic and personal service, 30 per cent, and the low per cent of 22 in manufacturing. Trade and transportation are both above the average in these cities, 20 per cent in trade and the quite high per cent of 17 in transportation. Physicians, lawyers, musicians, authors, electricians, and hairdressers are above average. The clergy are slightly underrepresented. Various governmental expenditures and taxes are high in these three cities.

Health Resorts

Some pleasure resorts are also health resorts. An effort was made to pick out some places known more as health resorts than as pleasure resorts. These were furnished by various physicians.[6] The places were small, the average being 15,500. Of the limited data on social characteristics, there seemed to be no distinguishing characteristics of these health resorts. The manufacturing wage may have been a little higher and there was no shortage of children. But the account of the health resorts was much like the account of the average city. Perhaps the proportion who seek these places because of health is too small to affect the social characteristics.

[5] Aiken, South Carolina; Asbury Park and Ocean City, New Jersey; Biloxi, Mississippi; Miami Beach, Daytona Beach, and Sarasota, Florida; Laconia, New Hampshire; Lake Geneva, Wisconsin; Newport, Rhode Island; Reno, Nevada; Santa Barbara, Monterey, and Santa Monica, California; Saratoga Springs and Lake Placid, New York; Swampscott, Massachusetts; Thomasville, Georgia.

[6] Colorado Springs, Colorado: Excelsior Springs, Missouri; Hendersonville, North Carolina; Hot Springs, Arkansas; Martinsville, Indiana; Mt. Clemens, Michigan; Rochester, Minnesota; Kerrville and San Angelo, Texas; Santa Fe, New Mexico; Saranac Lake, New York; Tucson, Arizona; Waukesha, Wisconsin.

Even the proportion of old persons is about the same as the average northern city but a little higher than in the average southern city.

COLLEGE TOWNS

There are a number of small places in the United States such as Princeton, New Jersey, where the college is the conspicuous feature of the town's life. Twenty-six such towns were chosen.[7] The average population was 13,700. The high percentage of school at-

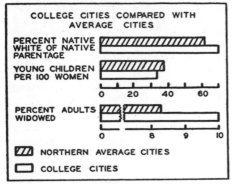

tendance is perhaps the most striking characteristic, as might be expected. Of the young persons 16 and 17 years of age 7 out of 10 are in school. The number of widowed persons is above average, 10 per cent. No doubt many widows move to these towns to educate their children and perhaps to take in roomers and boarders. Also the ratio of the old to the middle aged is high, 30, and of

[7] Ames, Iowa; Amherst and South Hadley, Massachusetts; Annapolis, Maryland; Ann Arbor, Michigan; Bloomington and Lafayette, Indiana; Boulder, Colorado; Bozeman, Montana; Champaign and Urbana, Illinois; Charlottesville, Virginia; Columbia, Missouri; Denton, Texas; Eugene, Oregon; Fayetteville, Arkansas; Tallahassee and Gainesville, Florida; Grinnell, and Iowa City, Iowa; Ithaca, New York; Lawrence, Kansas; Norman, Oklahoma; Oberlin, Ohio; Princeton, New Jersey; Tuscaloosa, Alabama.

the young is also high, 65. In other words the proportion of young adults and middle aged is small in contrast to the many of the other types of cities. The rent is about average, $28, contrary to popular opinion, perhaps because wages are not high. The average value of the owned home, $5,200, is a little above that for the average city, as is also the proportion of homes owned. The percentage of the population that are native whites of native born persons is 70, the highest of any type of city studied. The sex ratio of the single is the lowest for any of the cities already presented. There are only 93 single males to 100 single females, in contrast to 113 in the average city and 123 in the factory towns. This situation is probably due to the number of young women in the co-educational colleges. While the number of youth is large, the number of children under five years of age per 1,000 women 20 to 40 is slightly under the average.

In conclusion, it should be repeated that the degree of specialization of cities is probably found to be less when measured than is the popular opinion of it. Adjectives without any numerical checks often tend to exaggerate. Many cities are quite mixed as to the features of specialization especially if they are large. Thus places may be pleasure resorts and health resorts at the same time, or manufacturing towns and transportation centers. The foregoing selections tend toward single types of specialization though nearly all types of activities are represented in any one city. The number of trading centers and manufacturing towns greatly outnumber the other types. Very probably, then, these slight deviations one way or another from the average of the specialized cities would be much greater but in the same direction if specialization were more pronounced and there were less mixture of occupations in these cities.

CHAPTER X

SPECIALIZATION AND SUBURBAN DEVELOPMENT

*Here cities within metropolitan areas are compared with
an equal number of cities outside such areas with
regard to diversification in a variety of characteristics.*

SUBURBS are a creation of recent times. They are made possible by the abundance of rapid transportation. People can and do thus cluster outside the city's boundary line, drawn generally previous to the recent growth of transportation. There are many interesting phenomena about such aggregations of population hugging the highways or railways leading into a city or living in other cities adjacent to the larger city. One interesting question concerns the degree of the homogeneity or diversification of occupations and other characteristics.

One theory is that the suburban movement is simply an expansion of parts of the city outward and the suburbs are thus diversified just as are the wards within the city. In Chicago, for example, there are cities within the city, Polish, Bohemian, Italian, etc. Are not the suburbs a repetition of the same phenomena outside the city's gates rather than within them? This conception views suburbs as parts of a city in an economic sense as truly as any other part within the city limits. The reason they are not governmentally a part of the city is simply the lag of government in taking in these areas. The fact that Cleveland Heights is not a part of political Cleveland is an accident of government rather than a difference in economic and social independence.

If this conception be correct the suburbs should be highly heterogeneous; for they are like the different areas within the city. These local areas within the city have been frequently studied in the form of census tracts, wards, or local communities. They may be as different as Gold Coast and slum, as Bohemian quarter and a section made up largely of families with children, or as business district and residence district. If suburbs are simply an extension of this sort of urban differentiation they would be heterogeneous as are the various parts of a city.

Another theory of suburbs is that they are relatively homogeneous since their conditions of life are supposed to be much alike. The inhabitants are not crowded as in a city. They are likely to have the common characteristic of children and yards. They are more likely to be married couples in middle life. According to this theory even though they are socially and economically a part of a highly differentiated metropolis they are, nevertheless, it is argued, a homogeneous part. In a somewhat similar way, the slums, though located in different parts of a city, have many traits in common.

METHOD OF STUDY

These ideas about the nature of suburbs are such that they may be tested by the facts. But first there must be set up some standard of homogeneity with which to compare these satellite cities. One method is to select cities of the same size in the same region that are not in the orbit of the metropolis and then compare the heterogeneity of the satellite cities with these more traditional cities. This method does not compare the heterogeneity of the suburbs with local areas within the city. Such a comparison would be difficult to do statistically. But if the suburbs are more or less homogeneous than "normal" cities, we have at least information about the nature of suburbs by way of comparison and especially concerning whether the specialization pro-

[47]

cess which is taking place in cities is proceeding faster or slower in the suburban types. It is possible that the specialization movement is found furthest developed in these satellite cities.

The method of comparing the homogeneity of satellite cities with other cities may be illustrated by a case. The characteristics of monthly rent were chosen for study, and the average rents paid in each suburb were found. When these were grouped it was found that there were a good many wealthy suburbs where the average rent was high and also a good many working men's suburbs where the rent was low. On the other hand, the rents for a similar number of other cities not near big cities were collected and arranged on a scale; and it was found that most of these rents were nearly the same from one city to another. They thus tended to be close to the average. In the one case the rents were scattered and tended to cluster in two groups, the high rent suburbs and the low rent suburbs. In the other case they were not very scattered. There is a measure for this scatter which is called the standard deviation. In the case of the suburbs the standard deviation was $16, and in the case of the non-satellite cities the standard deviation measuring the variation was only $4.

The sizes of these standard deviations show then that for the attribute of rent there is more variation in the suburbs than in the non-suburbs. The conclusion is then drawn that in the case of rents there is more specialization in satellite cities than in cities not close to metropolises. In the matter of rent paid the non-satellite cities are more alike, while the suburbs are divided into rich men's suburbs and poor men's suburbs.

If another characteristic is studied, though, the result might not be the same. For instance, in regard to the employment of married women outside the home it would seem that the suburbs would be much alike in this characteristic, for probably many married women in suburbs have children and hence would find it difficult to work and care for children at the same time. On the other hand, cities in general may vary a good deal in the opportunities for women

working. In any case in a sample of cities and suburbs the standard deviation was smaller for the suburbs (3.4) than in the cities not close to a metropolis (4.6). There is then in regard to the employment of married women less variation in the suburbs than in the cities. It is obviously desirable to study a large number of characteristics to test these theories regarding the nature of suburbs.

In making such comparisons it is necessary to select comparable cities. For instance, one sample of places within the shopping areas of large cities included 25 suburbs, 13 in the Northeastern States, 9 in the Middle Western states, and 3 on the Pacific Coast. To compare with these, 25 cities without the shopping areas of large cities were chosen, with 13 in the Northeast, 9 in the Middle West, and 3 on the Pacific Coast. Each suburb was thus matched with a non-suburban city of about the same size. Thus Berkeley, California, 82,000 in population, was matched with Sacramento, California, with 93,000 population. The average population of this sample of suburbs was 65,000, and of all the cities in the sample without the shopping area was 67,000.

A similar process was followed for cities within the population group 25,000 to 50,000, which included 24 normal cities and 24 suburbs, and for a group of 31 suburbs and 31 non-suburban cities of a smaller size from 10,000 to 25,000 in population. With cities selected in this manner, there are three samples of cities within the shopping areas of big cities for three different sizes of places, and a similar number of cities without the shopping areas with about the same population and the same general location.

The method of testing whether there is more variation, and hence more specialization, in suburbs than in other similar cities is then clear. The results may now be examined. In types of occupation the suburbs are generally more varied. For percentages of the working population that are teachers, the standard deviations for two of the population classes of cities for the suburbs are 1.04 and .68 while for the other cities they are .42 and .45 (see Table I).

These measures mean that for the suburbs some have a very large per cent of teachers and some have a very small per cent, while for the comparable cities which are not suburban the percentage of teachers is more nearly the same. The suburbs are also more highly differentiated as to clergymen, police, and servants. But in respect to private guards and restaurant keepers the cities without the shopping areas are more different among themselves, as might be expected.

For indices having to do with income there is a much wider variation among the cities within the shopping radius. Such is the case in radios owned which was in 1930 something of an index of income, in percentage paying income taxes, in the average rents paid, in the average value of the homes owned, in wages in manufacturing, and in wages paid in retail stores. In regard to economic conditions, then, it is quite clear that the satellite cities are differentiated into the rich and the poor (in comparison with the wealthy suburbs), while the cities not near to big cities are more nearly like the average.

TABLE I

SPECIALIZATION IN SUBURBS

Social Characteristics	Diversification in Terms of Standard Deviations By Size of Cities					
	Populations in Thousands					
	Cities Within Metropolitan Areas			Cities Outside Metropolitan Areas		
	50-100	25-50	10-25	50-100	25-50	10-25
Teachers per 100 Workers	1.04	.68		.42	.45	
Clergymen	.09	.07		.09	.05	
Police	.14	.10		.10	.05	
Guards	.17	.00		.28	.10	
Hotel and Restaurant Keepers	.17	.20		.20	.28	
Personal and Domestic Service Workers	4.33	3.63		4.04	2.11	
Radios, Per Cent of Families Owning	13.67	9.45	13.14	7.00	9.05	11.75
Income Tax Payers, Per Cent of Adults	4.63	2.90	5.67	1.51	2.09	2.07
Median Monthly Rental	16.05	13.13	12.80	4.28	5.04	5.40
Median Value of Homes	3,660	3,366	3,571	1,420	1,331	1,150
Annual Earnings Rate, Manufacturing	236	183	341	204	182	199
Annual Earnings Rate, Retail	138	136	164	120	102	159
Married, Per Cent of Adults	3.87	3.92	5.61	3.62	4.18	3.30
Widowers, Per Cent of Adults	.66	.81	.98	.67	.32	.73
Widows, Per Cent of Adults	2.84	2.38	2.61	1.70	1.37	2.30
Median Size of Family	.35	.32	.30	.27	.25	.23
Families With No Young Children (in per cents)	8.65	6.27	6.78	5.32	3.70	4.82
Children under Five per 100 Married Women	9.30	9.98		8.30	8.16	
Married Women Employed (in per cents)	4.02	3.35		4.08	4.62	
Home Owners, Per Cent of Families	10.86	9.43	10.32	9.82	7.11	7.44
Apartment Houses, Per Cent of Dwellings	5.99	5.01	2.09	5.74	3.46	1.21
Families with Lodgers (in per cents)	5.06	2.88		2.15	2.64	
Sex Ratio of Single Men to Single Women	50.25	25.35	33.60	22.95	29.70	71.60
Single Men, 20-35 (in per cents)	2.96	1.92		1.70	2.00	
Single Women, 20-35 (in per cents)	2.77	2.60		2.30	2.32	
Debt Per Capita	74.39	65.44		33.54	33.22	
Taxes Per Capita	26.70	24.90		9.97	6.89	
Cost of Health Per Capita	.36	.44		.37	.32	
Cost of Courts Per Capita	.17	.20		.09	.10	
Cost of Libraries Per Capita	.46	.39		.32	.20	
Cost of Recreation Per Capita	.84	1.36		.67	.60	
Foreign-born Whites (in per cents)	11.96	10.09	7.26	8.62	8.85	8.19
School Attendance at 16-17 (in per cents)	18.03	18.44	19.52	16.73	16.43	12.37
Young Persons as Ratio to Middle Aged	13.20	10.30	11.04	9.48	10.22	9.72
Old Persons as Ratio to Middle Aged	.09	.06	.07	.07	.04	.07
Children, 10-15, Employed (in per cents)	.24	1.41		.87	.90	

In regard to conditions of family life and organization, the suburbs are more varied as to average size of family. There are suburbs with large families and suburbs with small families, whereas the non-suburban cities are more nearly average. There is also slightly more variation in the suburbs in the percentage of the population married, which is somewhat contrary to popular opinion. With regard to children an index was computed showing the number of children under 5 years of age per 100 married women. The suburbs are again more varied, as is also the case with the number of families with no children under ten years of age living at home. These conclusions do not support the theory that family life is more homogeneous in the suburbs. There is a good deal of interest in regard to the data on families in the suburbs, since popular writers have claimed that the matriarchate, once supposed to have been widely spread among primitive peoples, is being reestablished in the suburbs. For are not the men away at work in another city, and the women left in power in the suburban home? If this were the case there would probably be more uniformity in the suburban sample as to family characteristics, which there is not. On the other hand, the variation in the percentage of married women at work is greater in the non-suburban cities. The same is true of all women at work, whether married or not.

In many other categories dealing with conditions relating to family the diversification is greater within the suburbs, as, for instance, families living in owned homes, families living in apartments; families taking in lodgers, and in the percentage of single women 20 to 35 years of age. In the ratio of single men to single women, however, there is more uniformity in the suburbs. In general, it is seen that in the conditions of family life and conditions related thereto these suburbs are more diversified, as is known to be the case with the various local communities within the city limits of very large cities.

Another battery of characteristics has been found concerning government. There is more heterogeneity among the suburbs in per capita indebtedness of the government and in the per capita taxes than in the case of the independent cities. These cities outside the trading areas are also more unlike in the cost of certain governmental services as those providing recreation, libraries, health conditions, and courts.

For certain miscellaneous traits, it is noted that in the number of foreign-born persons the suburbs are more different among themselves, as though some of them specialize in having immigrants and others specialize in not having them. For the control group of cities there is more uniformity. In the employment of children the larger suburbs have child labor and less variation among them in this trait. But the opposite is true for the medium sized cities. The diversification in school attendance is greater in the suburbs when measured by the percentage of the children 16 and 17 years of age that are in school. With regard to the age of the population, suburbs are less homogeneous than the cities independent of the great metropolitan centers. Some seem to have more old and some less old; some more young and some less young.

Cities within the metropolitan area have been compared with an equal number without the area, comparable in size and regional location, with regard to diversification in a variety of characteristics. The suburbs specialize more in these various traits than do the cities more independent of larger cities. For the three different classes of cities there were 91 different comparisons as to variability. In 72 of these 91, or 80 per cent of the comparisons, there was greater diversification among the suburbs. It is concluded then that the specialization process taking place in cities goes further in the satellite cities. These are generally the newer and more rapidly growing cities and hence have more of an opportunity to specialize. But the specialization is probably not caused by growth; growth rather extends the opportunity. The reason for the specialization is probably the same as that which causes certain blocks within a city to specialize, since the satellite cities seem to be more or less an extension of these specialized city blocks outward beyond the official city limits.

CHAPTER XI

HOW SATELLITE CITIES DIFFER FROM OTHERS

On the basis of an analysis of 20 satellite cities, this chapter indicates in what ways and to what degree they differ from other cities.

SINCE the beginning of the twentieth century satellite cities have experienced a rapid growth. Their development is correlated with the increasing use of the automobile and the truck. Their populations have come from places outside the metropolitan shopping area, but also from the metropolis itself.

The inventions which have aided the growth of satellite cities have been made use of by various social forces, such as manufacturing industries seeking lower wages, lower rents, and lower taxes and by families who wanted more play space for children and lower rents.

The influence of all these various inventions and social forces which have created these new cities contiguous to larger cities has not yet spent itself. There is reason then to think that the satellite cities will continue to increase in number and some of them in size.

It has been shown in a previous article that satellite cities have tended to specialize more than other cities outside the sphere of influence of the metropolis. Are there other differences between the newer satellite cities and the older less specialized cities? Is the satellite city a new type of city? Since there are likely to be many more of them, will they add any new characteristics to our urban population?

METHOD OF COMPARISON

The following paragraphs are devoted to an attempt to find out in what ways and to what degree satellite cities differ from other cities. One method will be to study the average satellite city, not the various types, and to compare the results with the average non-satellite city. In this way light may be thrown on the theories that the suburbs are bedroom cities, that there are more children in them, that there are more women, that there are more servants, that there are fewer common laborers, etc.

The average suburb was determined from a selection of satellite cities[1] from which very wealthy suburbs were excluded and the industrial ones also. All suburbs with homes of an average value of $10,000 or more or a monthly rental of $50 and over were excluded. The population range was kept around 50,000; indeed the average population was 47,400. These cities were from the Northeast and West, hence a very good selection to compare with the average city discussed previously. The average city referred to was based on cities from the Northeast and West, the cities from the South being omitted. The size was about the same as that of the satellite cities.

Another method was slightly different. In a previous discussion showing that suburbs were more specialized than cities of the same size and region but outside the metropolitan shopping area, the variations of cities within and without the shopping areas were compared. These same cities may be compared not only as to variation but also as to average characteristics. The second method will

[1] Alameda, Alhambra, and Glendale, California; Arlington, Malden, Medford, Quincy, and Watertown, Massachusetts; Belleville, Bloomfield, Irvington, Orange, and Plainfield, New Jersey; Cranston, Rhode Island; East Cleveland and Norwood, Ohio; Berwyn and Maywood, Illinois; West Haven, Connecticut; and Wilkinsburg, Pennsylvania.

prove to be a check on the first, so that it should be possible to delineate the characteristics of the satellite city quite definitively.

OCCUPATIONS

The average satellite city has a much larger per cent of its working population engaged in clerical occupations than is found in the average city; in fact the per cent is nearly three quarters greater in the suburbs. Why this is so is not known, unless persons following this line of occupations do more commuting. There is not much difference in the numbers following trade and manufacturing pursuits. Transportation occupations seem to be less numerous in the suburbs; and, strange to say, so are the numbers in the domestic and personal service occupations. Hotel and restaurant keepers are to be found in smaller numbers in the satellite cities, as would be expected. There are more police per unit of working population in the satellite cities than in other cities. Perhaps the crime is also less, though no data were compiled on this topic. The per cent who are clergymen is about 25 per cent less in the average satellite city than in other cities. There is also a larger per cent of teachers generally in the satellite cities. Not much difference exists in the numbers

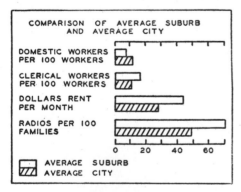

of lawyers, physicians, and musicians.

Such then are the differences in occupations. No outstanding principle seems to be discernible from the averages.

ECONOMIC CONDITIONS

The economic conditions in the suburbs appear to be more favorable than in other

cities. Comparisons between the average suburb and the average city as to economic conditions are not very reliable because of the method used in picking the sample on which the average suburb was based. It is recalled that an attempt was made to exclude the wealthy suburb and the working men's suburbs. In excluding these a line was drawn somewhat arbitrarily regarding wealth which, of course, affects the section when economic conditions are considered. The data, however, are rather convincing when suburbs of different sizes were compared with cities of the same size and same region but outside the metropolitan area. This comparison seems a fair one and not biased in selection so far as could be determined. The number making income tax returns is higher in the suburbs. The annual rates of earnings in manufacturing and in stores were higher in the satellite cities, whatever their size.

The average rents paid were higher as was also the value of owned homes. The rents may be lower in the suburb than in the adjoining metropolis but not lower than in a city of the same size not in the metropolitan area. The number of families having radios was larger in the satellite cities by 15 or 20 per cent. Why should the suburbs show more favorable economic conditions? Do wealthier residents of the metropolis move into the suburbs to live? Or are the conditions of marketing more favorable in the shopping area of the big cities? Whatever may be the reason, favorable economic conditions may be the explanation of the greater rate of growth of satellite cities.

FAMILY LIFE

The percentage of the population married is greater in the suburbs. It seems reasonable to think that this fact represents a selection. There is probably a tendency for the married to move to the suburbs. On the other hand there is a slightly larger percentage of single men 20 to 35 years of age in the satellite cities than in the cities without the trading area. This is also the case for single women of the same age, though the number of single men and single women in the metropolis is probably larger. How can there be both

DIFFERENCES BETWEEN SATELLITE CITIES AND OTHERS

SOCIAL CHARACTERISTICS	COMPARISONS IN TERMS OF AVERAGES BY SIZE OF CITIES Population in Thousands					
	Cities Within Metropolitan Areas			Cities Outside Metropolitan Areas		
	50-100	25-50	10-25	50-100	25-50	10-25
Teachers per 100 Workers	2.45	2.26		2.30	2.27	
Clergymen	.24	.23		.30	.28	
Police	.40	.35		.33	.29	
Guards	.37	.36		.40	.10	
Hotel and Restaurant Keepers	.41	.42		.48	.58	
Personal and Domestic Service Workers	10.39	9.61		9.62	10.50	
Radios, Per Cent of Families Owning	61.60	63.20	61.44	49.81	47.24	43.33
Income Tax Payers, Per Cent of Adults	9.12	8.22	10.16	7.58	6.52	7.34
Median Monthly Rental	43.80	38.53	36.82	28.62	27.21	25.82
Median Value of Homes	7,360	8,000	7,613	5,740	5,250	4,468
Annual Earnings Rate, Manufacturing	1,580	1,420	1,520	1,310	1,310	1,250
Annual Earnings Rate, Retail	1,520	1,470	1,460	1,390	1,320	1,380
Married, Per Cent of Adults	60.50	61.70	62.12	59.64	60.84	60.00
Widowers, Per Cent of Adults	3.60	3.90	3.77	4.60	4.59	4.50
Widows, Per Cent of Adults	10.46	10.89	10.85	11.15	11.47	11.08
Median Size of Family	3.54	3.49	3.51	3.50	3.41	3.42
Children Under Five per 100 Married Women	52.71	53.23		56.72	54.85	
Families With no Young Children (in per cents)	60.95	61.19	60.40	62.13	63.58	62.10
Married Women Employed (in per cents)	11.61	11.83		13.76	14.14	
Home Owners, Per Cent of Families	43.36	49.37	56.08	48.51	50.40	49.76
Apartment Houses, Per Cent of Dwellings	6.86	4.79	1.93	4.43	2.85	2.23
Families with Lodgers (in per cents)	11.63	9.12		10.30	10.58	
Sex Ratio of Single Men to Single Women	129.16	114.22	121.10	111.56	125.26	134.78
Single Men, 20-35 (in per cents)	17.10	15.33		14.50	13.85	
Single Women, 20-35 (in per cents)	11.29	10.83		10.98	9.86	
Debt Per Capita	113.10	109.00		79.54	68.78	
Taxes Per Capita	63.87	59.68		50.99	43.47	
Cost of Health Per Capita	.80	.70		.69	.64	
Cost of Courts Per Capita	.23	.23		.13	.18	
Cost of Libraries Per Capita	.73	.58		.54	.51	
Cost of Recreation Per Capita	1.21	1.47		1.02	.94	
Foreign-born Whites (in per cents)	21.3	17.5	14.3	14.7	12.8	10.4
School Attendance at 16-17 (in per cents)	64.50	64.31	70.93	63.06	63.76	67.85
Young Persons as Ratio to Middle Aged	63.80	64.50	67.40	69.30	67.20	68.70
Old Persons as Ratio to Middle Aged	.21	.24	.24	.26	.27	.26
Children, 10-15, Employed (in per cents)	1.4	1.6		1.7	1.3	

larger percentages of the married and also of the single in the suburbs at the same time? This can be true if there are smaller percentages of widowed in suburbs, which is the case. There are fewer widowed perhaps because there are fewer old people. Suburbs are generally younger cities and tend to have fewer old people, since in general it is not the old people who migrate to the newer places.

The evidence is quite conclusive that the family is larger in the suburbs. There are fewer families of one and two persons only and more families with more than five persons. Also fewer families are found in the suburbs with no children under 10 years of age. With regard to homes it is generally assumed that there are fewer apartments as compared with single family dwellings in the suburbs. Such may be the case in comparison with the metropolis to which the suburb is satellite. But there are more apartment houses in the satellite cities than in other cities without the metropolitan orbit, and the average suburb has more apartments than the average city of the same size which is not a suburb. This larger number of apartments may be due to the recency of building construction in the suburbs. There does not seem to be much difference as to the degree of home ownership even though there be more apartments in satellite cities.

As to the employment of married women, there is less in the satellite cities, as would be expected since the family is larger. There are, however, fewer very little children (under five years of age) per 100 married women in the satellite cities than in other cities, though there may be more than in the metropolis. It may be possible that migration to the suburb does not occur until the baby has grown older. There are fewer females employed and also fewer families with lodgers in the satellite cities.

In general the suburbs present a picture of more family life than does the average city or place of similar size outside the shopping areas of big cities. The conditions of family life seem more nearly normal except in two instances. There is a larger percentage of single and also a smaller percentage of little children under five years of age.

GOVERNMENT

There has been a good deal of discussion about governments of suburbs. Where satel-

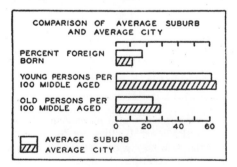

lite cities are strictly contiguous or very close to larger cities, there is argument for economies arising from consolidation and for some gain in efficiency, as perhaps in police and fire service. For the cities under discussion, taxes are a good deal higher in the satellite cities than in the other cities not near to the metropolis, whatever be the comparison with the metropolis. So also the gov-

ernmental expenditures for certain services such as health, schools, courts, libraries, and recreation are greater in the satellite cities. Perhaps the developments in the metropolis of governmental functions are more readily

COMPARISON OF AVERAGE SUBURBS AND AVERAGE CITIES

SOCIAL CHARACTERISTICS	Average Suburb	Average City
Teachers per 100 Workers	2.52	2.38
Clergy	.20	.31
Police	.39	.29
Officials and Inspectors	.31	.37
Physicians	.33	.39
Lawyers	.45	.42
Authors	.20	.16
Musicians	.50	.48
Electricians	1.03	.72
Hairdressers	.86	1.04
Miners	.16	.82
Public Service Workers	2.00	2.00
Personal and Domestic Service Workers	8.1	11.6
Clerks	17.0	10.7
Factory Workers	35.0	37.0
Trade Workers	18.0	17.0
Transportation Workers	7.8	9.8
Professional Workers	9.9	8.7
Taxes Per Adult	60.1	42.7
Debt Per Capita	89.9	69.6
School Cost Per Adult	27.9	23.3
School Cost Per Student	81.1	78.5
Health Cost Per Capita	.72	.49
Library Cost Per Capita	.58	.58
Recreation Cost Per Capita	1.16	1.30
Radios, % of Families Owning	71.0	49.0
Median Monthly Rental	44.0	28.0
Median Value of Homes	8,400	5,000
Annual Earnings Rate, Mfg	1,390	1,300
Annual Earnings Rate, Retail	1,480	1,350
Married, % of Adults	62.0	60.0
Widowed, % of Adults	7.5	8.3
Median Size of Family, Minus Families of One	3.45	3.33
Apartment Houses, % of Dwellings	4.1	2.5
Home Owners, % of Families	50.0	50.0
Families with no Young Children	62.0	65.0
Home Makers Employed, in %	12.2	15.2
Sex Ratio of Single Men to Single Women	105.0	116.0
Married Women Employed, in %	11.0	13.0
Families with 2 or More Persons Employed	34.0	31.0
Children Under Five per 100 Married Women	37.5	38.3
Families With Lodgers, in %	9.0	10.4
Women Employed, % over Fifteen	25.0	26.0
Foreign-born Whites, in %	17.0	12.0
Native Whites of Native Parents, in %	45.0	62.0
Young Persons as Ratio to Middle Aged	.62	.64
Old Persons as Ratio to Middle Aged	.24	.29
School Attendance at 16-17, in %	67.	68.

diffused into the suburbs than into further outlying cities, and perhaps the favorable economic factors encourage the growth of such social services.

MISCELLANEOUS

There are some other characteristics of suburbs that might be noted. One is the larger percentage of foreign-born white in the average suburbs than in the average city and than in comparable cities outside the metropolitan orbit. This fact may be surprising; but if the satellite city populations come more largely from the metropolis then the larger number of foreign-born whites may not be unexpected. There are more foreign-born whites, even though the per cent engaged in manufacturing is less in the suburbs.

An important characteristic of populations is age. In this study a group from 20 to 55 years old in age has been segregated and called here the middle aged, though this is not quite the common usage of the term. The suburbs have a larger percentage of these middle-aged persons than have other cities. Hence there are fewer old persons and somewhat fewer persons under 20, although it has been shown that the suburbs are favorable to children. This high per-

centage of middle-aged adults is often a phenomenon of migration. That is, cities which are growing most rapidly are likely to have fewer very young persons and fewer elders. In the course of time this age distribution changes, so that there are more old and more very young. Such may be the case with suburbs. Some of the characteristics previously described flow from this skewed age distribution in the suburbs.

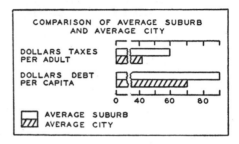

In conclusion, then, though there are many distinguishing characteristics of satellite cities, perhaps the outstanding ones are the high percentage in the clerical occupations, the low percentage of the clergy, the favorable economic conditions, the more adequate support of government, the small number of old people, and the more normal family life.

CHAPTER XII

WEALTHY SUBURBS AND INDUSTRIAL SUBURBS

The amount of income is a powerful factor in producing social differences in occupations, population characteristics, and governmental activities of wealthy, as compared with industrial, suburbs.

OF THE various types of suburbs, two are fairly common. One is the wealthy suburb, of which illustrations are Rye, New York, Shaker Heights, Ohio, and Beverly Hills, California. The other type found near many big cities is the industrial suburb with factories and many workmen. Such are Camden, New Jersey, Homestead, Pennsylvania, and River Rouge, Michigan. These types might be called rich and poor suburbs, except that. the industrial suburbs are poor only relatively to the wealthy suburbs. The wage earners in many of them receive higher than average wages. Cities that are not suburbs hardly present such contrasts. Sections within a city often do, but adequate data about enough of them are not available, whereas the census does publish for these suburbs sufficient data to paint a very good picture of the type of social life found in working men's suburbs and in places in which are the homes of the wealthy. The cleavage is not so sharp as the previous sentence indicates, for many persons with low incomes live in wealthy suburbs, and there are some fine homes in industrial suburbs, especially when the suburbs are large. So the actual differences understate the real differences between the social surroundings of the rich and of the working men.

The contrasting pictures of the wealthy suburbs and the industrial suburbs afford many interesting speculations. A higher standard of living is the great desideratum of the human race. Does the chart of the wealthy suburb show what the working men are struggling for and have not obtained? As the standard of living is raised for the working man will he move in the direction of the attainments of the wealthy suburb? The following comparisons are not like photographs. But the statistics reveal observations which a camera would not catch.

METHOD

The method is not to compare individual cities, for each city has local peculiarities. It is better to compare averages even if the contrasts are less vivid. The first step was to select the industrial suburbs. These were defined as places with more than 45 or 50 per cent of their population engaged in manufacturing, and with no more than the average proportion in trade and in transportation, Twenty-nine[1] such factory towns were studied. Their average population in 1930 was 48,300 and they were largely in the Northeastern and the Middle Western parts of the United States.

The wealthy suburbs were approximately of the same size; 53,300 was the average number of inhabitants, but they were fewer in number, only ten.[2]

---

[1] Amsterdam, New York; Bayonne, Camden, Clifton, Garfield, Perth Amboy, Passaic, and Kearney, New Jersey; Central Falls, East Providence, Pawtucket, and Woonsocket, Rhode Island; Cicero, Granite City, and Waukegan, Illinois; Chester and McKeesport, Pennsylvania; East Chicago, Hammond, and Mishawaka, Indiana; Chicopee, Holyoke, and Salem, Massachusetts; Massillon and Warren, Ohio; West Allis, Wisconsin; Dearborn, Hamtramck, and Wyandotte, Michigan.

[2] Brookline and Newton, Massachusetts; Cleveland Heights and Lakewood, Ohio; East Orange and Montclair, New Jersey; Evanston and Oak Park, Illinois; University City, Missouri; and White Plains, New York.

Suburbs were rated as wealthy suburbs where the median value of homes was over $10,000 and where the median monthly rent was over $50. The actual average median value was $15,000, while in the industrial suburbs the average value was $6,800. The average median monthly rent in the wealthy suburb was $69 a month and in the industrial suburb $32. It may be noted that in the industrial suburbs the value of homes and rents were higher than in the average city. Let us see how the averages of the two types of suburbs compare.

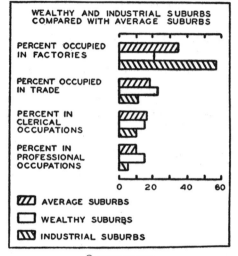

WEALTHY AND INDUSTRIAL SUBURBS COMPARED WITH AVERAGE SUBURBS

PERCENT OCCUPIED IN FACTORIES

PERCENT OCCUPIED IN TRADE

PERCENT IN CLERICAL OCCUPATIONS

PERCENT IN PROFESSIONAL OCCUPATIONS

0   20   40   60

AVERAGE SUBURBS

WEALTHY SUBURBS

INDUSTRIAL SUBURBS

OCCUPATIONS

The wealthy suburbs have a minimum of manufacturing, only 21 per cent of their working population were in manufacturing as compared with 57 per cent in the industrial suburbs. They both have few in transportation and in public service. In the wealthy suburbs 15 per cent are in the clerical occupations as compared with 10 per cent in the factory towns. Those at work furnishing domestic and personal services are more than twice as numerous in the richer communities, 17 per cent to 7 per cent. The most striking difference in occupations however is the very large percentage of professional men and women in the wealthy suburbs, 15 per cent, which is three times the percentage in the professions in the working men's communities. The professions furnish a very high type of personal service which is generally quite costly and can be purchased much more readily by the rich than by the poor. Of course, it is quite possible that many of the professional men and women may only live in the suburbs but have offices in the neighboring metropolis.

In every type of profession there are more in the wealthy neighborhoods than in the industrial suburbs. The percentage of physicians, .86, is 4 times as great. The proportion of lawyers, 1.45, is 6 times as large. The clergy, .27, are about half again as numerous. The teachers, 3.44, are just double; while the percentage of musicians, .67, is a little more than double that found in the industrial suburbs. These facts may not mean that the wealthy command the services of these professions from two to six times as much as the working men. The professional men and women may merely prefer to have the rich as neighbors and are able to do so.

The number of police is about the same in the two types of suburbs, but the number of officials, inspectors and private guards is larger in the wealthy communities. The picture of the occupations in the two places then is that of one community with a limited number of personal services and the other with an extraordinarily large amount of them.

POPULATION CHARACTERISTICS

In the industrial suburbs only 1 inhabitant in 3 is native born white of native parents. Yet, in the wealthy suburbs the ratio is only 1 in 2. There are also more than the average number of foreign-born white in the wealthy suburbs, 1 in 6 as compared with 1 in 4 in the factory towns. In smaller suburbs of 15,000 inhabitants, the differences were not so great, about 1 in 6 in each. It should be said that some data are available for small suburbs under 25,000. In general, the smaller the place, the less heterogeneous it probably is, and the smaller the chance for extraneous characteristics to be found. It is regretted that more data are not available for the small places. Occasional reference will be made to these smaller places. As regards race and stock in the population, the averages would be different no doubt, if suburbs from the Southern states had been included.

The wealthy suburbs have a good many old people. This is probably to be expected, since the wealthy are better able than the wage earners to care for the old. The old are here defined as those being over 55 years of age; and their ratio to the young and middle-aged adults, 20 to 55 years of age, is in the wealthy suburbs 27 to 100 as compared with 18 among the wage earners. The industrial communities attract young able-bodied workers and probably have little use for the older persons, who may go back to farms or villages.

With regard to the young, that is, those below 20 years of age, the wealthy suburbs have less than the average, while the industrial suburbs have more than the average. The ratio which the youth is to the young and middle aged is 53 and 77 to 100 respectively for the two types of communities. The average age in the industrial suburbs must be quite a good deal lower than that in the wealthy suburbs.

A very spectacular difference is the large number of unmarried young men in the industrial cities and the large number of unmarried young women in the wealthy communities. Such facts are usually expressed in a figure known as the sex ratio which is the number of males to 100 females. The sex ratio is about the same for children and for married persons but may differ a great deal among the single. In the working men's districts here studied, there are 137 single men to 100 single women, while in the wealthy neighborhoods the sex ratio is only 75. This difference would seem to be a phenomenon of migration, not of the birth rate nor of the death rate. Industry draws young men, and the wealthy can take care of the young women or employ them as servants. This distribution of the sexes among rich and poor is a fairly common observation.

FAMILY

Among the wage earners there is a larger percentage married, 61 per cent of those over 15 years of age, as compared with 59 per cent in the more prosperous communities. These percentages may be affected by dif-

ferences in age distribution. There are more widows in the richer communities, 8 per cent as compared with 6 per cent in the industrial communities. This observation is quite characteristic of distributions of population based on wealth. The family among wage earning communities is about 12 per cent

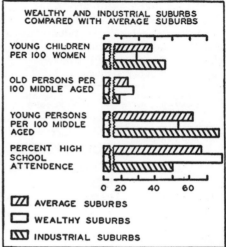

larger than in the wealthy suburbs, even though the well-to-do may have more relatives living in the household. The difference in the size of the family is probably due to differences in the birth rate. The birth rates are not always accurate because of hospital births, so sometimes the number of children under 5 years of age per 100 women, 20 to 44 years of age, is used as a comparative index of the birth rate. The number of such little children is very much higher in the industrial suburbs, 46 to 28. This larger number of very young children may not be due wholly to the birth rate; it may be that the married women are younger in the industrial suburbs. The number of families with no children under 10 years of age is much greater in the wealthy suburbs. Thus one sees many more little children in the factory towns.

Families with lodgers are more numerous in the factory towns as is also the percentage of married women at work. The proportion of females at work, however, is larger in the wealthy suburbs, possibly because of more servants in the wealthy neighborhoods.

Quite an impressive difference is the greater attendance at high school in the wealthier places. Of the boys and girls 16 and 17 years of age in 1930, 78 per cent were in high school. This is really quite a high percentage, nearly 4 out of every 5; while in the wage earners' towns, only 55 per cent, or little better than 1 in 2 are in school.

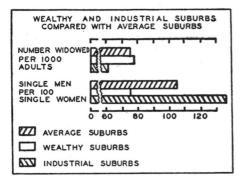

WEALTHY AND INDUSTRIAL SUBURBS COMPARED WITH AVERAGE SUBURBS

NUMBER WIDOWED PER 1000 ADULTS

SINGLE MEN PER 100 SINGLE WOMEN

0 60 80 100 120

AVERAGE SUBURBS
WEALTHY SUBURBS
INDUSTRIAL SUBURBS

As to radios in homes in 1930, 78 per cent of the families had them in the rich suburbs and 54 per cent in the poorer ones. Curiously, there is not much difference in the extent of home ownership—46 per cent in the factory towns and 49 per cent in the wealthy suburbs. So slight a difference is unexpected, and a possible explanation does not come readily to mind.

The family in the wealthy suburbs is smaller, older, living in better houses, with more widowed persons and females, and undoubtedly more servants, while the family in the industrial suburbs is younger, with more little children, less school attendance, with more home-makers employed outside the home, with more families taking in lodgers, and with more members of the family at work outside the home.

COMPARISON OF WEALTHY SUBURBS AND INDUSTRIAL SUBURBS

SOCIAL CHARACTERISTICS	WEALTHY SUBURBS	INDUSTRIAL SUBURBS
Teachers per 100 Workers..	3.44	1.77
Clergymen	.27	.19
Police	.37	.36
Officials and Inspectors	.29	.18
Physicians	.86	.21
Lawyers	1.45	.24
Authors	.40	.09

COMPARISON OF WEALTHY SUBURBS AND INDUSTRIAL SUBURBS—Continued

SOCIAL CHARACTERISTICS	WEALTHY SUBURBS	INDUSTRIAL SUBURBS
Musicians	.67	.25
Electricians	.51	.90
Hairdressers	.57	.79
Miners	.09	.16
Public Service Workers	1.6	1.8
Personal and Domestic Service Workers	16.5	7.0
Clerks	15.4	10.0
Factory Workers	21.0	57.0
Trade Workers	23.0	11.0
Transportation Workers	5.9	6.5
Professional Workers	15.4	5.5
Taxes Per Adult	72.8	54.7
Debt Per Capita	135.6	122.8
School Cost Per Adult	34.4	30.4
School Cost Per Student	107.2	73.4
Health Cost Per Capita	.99	.75
Library Cost Per Capita	1.16	.53
Recreation Cost Per Capita	2.04	.86
Radios, % of Families Owning	78.0	54.0
Median Monthly Rental	69.0	32.0
Median Value of Homes	$15,000	$6,800
Annual Earnings Rate, Mfg.	$1,580	$1,440
Annual Earnings Rate, Retail	$1,580	$1,460
Married, % of Adults	59.0	61.0
Widowed, % of Adults	7.8	6.2
Median Size of Family, Minus Families of One	3.38	3.81
Apartment Houses, % of Dwellings	7.0	6.5
Home Owners, % of Families	49.0	46.0
Families with No Young Children, in %	66.0	55.0
Home Makers Employed, in %	11.7	13.2
Sex Ratio of Single Men to Single Women	75.0	137.0
Married Women Employed, in %	11.0	12.0
Families with 2 or More Persons Employed	30.0	38.0
Children under 5 per 100 Married Women	28.2	45.9
Families with Lodgers, in %	9.5	11.3
Women Employed, % over 15	29.0	25.0
School Attendance at 16-17 in %	78.0	50.0
Foreign-born Whites, in %	17.0	25.0
Native Whites, of Native Parents, in %	49.0	33.0
Young Persons as Ratio to Middle Aged	.53	.77
Old Persons as Ratio to Middle Aged	.27	.18

GOVERNMENTAL ACTIVITIES

In the wealthier suburbs more is spent for government as would be expected. The taxes per adult 15 years of age and over are $73 as compared with $55 in the industrial suburbs. The house rent is twice as much but the taxes are not. On education the wealthy suburbs spend $107 per pupil as compared with $73 in the industrial suburbs. The governmental expenditure for health purposes is one-fourth greater in the wealthy suburbs. For libraries it is twice as great and for recreational activities paid for by governments, which include parks and boulevards, the expenditure is almost three times as great in the wealthy suburbs as in the industrial ones. The per capita indebtedness of the city government is slightly greater in the wealthy suburbs, $136 to $123, but the ratio of indebtedness to taxation is not so great.

In conclusion, it may be said that not all of the differences cited are due to income, but most of them probably are. The study of these two types of suburbs shows what a powerful factor is income in producing social differences. It is obvious from these percentages that the higher incomes bring many community advantages.

CHAPTER XIII

INCREASING AND DECREASING CITIES

"Characteristics that are peculiar to increasing and decreasing cities seem to be related to the two factors of increased opportunity for income and migration."

JAMES BRYCE in his *American Commonwealth* writes of the optimism of the inhabitants in the growing cities of the West. If the growth is very rapid, there is a spirit of optimism so extreme that it may become one of recklessness. Bankruptcy is said to mean less in a rapidly growing city because it is easier to get on one's feet again. There is more boldness in undertaking new business ventures. If the place is extremely new, as well as rapidly growing, law and order are said to be less secure.

By contrast, it is said that cities that are losing population have a touch of sadness about them. At least there seems to be missing the spirit of buoyancy. It is difficult to undertake many expansion movements such as improving the schools when the tax base, that is, the population, is decreasing. No doubt the people are more careful, and it has been said the spirit of gaiety is less noticeable.

These are impressions. They may be true but they are not based on records, for the census takers do not have any questions on optimism and there are no statistics on sadness, though it would seem highly probable that the social atmosphere of declining cities is different from that of growing cities. Though these popular impressions are not readily subject to measurement, they do at least suggest that the statistics available might be looked into to see if any differences will be found.

The subject may be important, for the reason that the rate of population increase for the United States as a whole is markedly slowing up. This is very significant, for throughout the history of this country there has been an increasing population, with the correlated attitudes of hope, progress, expansion, and enterprise. Should the population of this nation become stationary in numbers or decrease, it seems probable that there will be corresponding changes in attitudes. This general population movement is already affecting cities, many of which are experiencing a slowing up of increase in population. With returning recovery, cities will continue to grow but undoubtedly less rapidly, and many of them will experience decreases in population. There are many probable social consequences that will flow from these changes, and some of them could probably be stated with fair assurance by deduction. But the purpose here is rather to see what the readily available facts will show as to the differences between certain cities that in 1930 showed losses or gains in population.

TABLE I

CITIES DECREASING IN POPULATION

City	Rate of Change 1910-1920	Rate of Change 1920-1930
Bay City, Michigan	5	0
Passaic, New Jersey	17	—1
Johnstown, Pennsylvania	21	—1
Fitchburg, Massachusetts	9	—1
Manchester, New Hampshire	12	—2
Newport News, Virginia	11	—9
Wilmington, Delaware	26	—3
Brockton, Massachusetts	17	—4
Fall River, Massachusetts		—4
Butte, Montana	6	—5
Holyoke, Massachusetts	4	—6
New Bedford, Massachusetts	25	—7
Charleston, South Carolina	16	—8
Petersburg, Virginia	29	—8
Superior, Wisconsin	—2	—9
Newport, Rhode Island	11	—9
Lawrence, Massachusetts	10	—10
Haverhill, Massachusetts	22	—10
Lowell, Massachusetts	6	—11
Hoboken, New Jersey	—3	—13
Portsmouth, Virginia	64	—16

METHOD

First, cities were selected which decreased in population from 1920 to 1930 and which showed from 1910 to 1920 either no decrease or a smaller increase than in the preceding decade. Only cities of a single population class were selected. The average population in 1930 was 63,000. There were 21 cities, with an average decrease of 6 per cent during the decade (see Table I).

A similar list of cities was selected which experienced an increase in population from 1920 to 1930 which was greater than the increase from 1910 to 1920. The average size was 50,000, and the number was 20, with an average rate of increase of 69 per cent during the decade 1920 to 1930. In general those cities were chosen which had a rather large increase (see Table 2).

TABLE 2

CITIES INCREASING IN POPULATION

CITY	RATE OF CHANGE 1910-1920	RATE OF CHANGE 1920-1930
Zanesville, Ohio	56	23
La Crosse, Wisconsin	0	30
Elgin, Illinois	6	31
Hamilton, Ohio	13	32
Altoona, Pennsylvania	16	36
Michigan City, Indiana	2	37
Peoria, Illinois	14	38
Newton, Massachusetts	16	42
Springfield, Missouri	13	45
South Bend, Indiana	32	47
Parkersburg, West Virginia	12	48
Bloomfield, New Jersey	46	73
Waukegan, Illinois	20	74
Albuquerque, New Mexico	38	75
Clifton, New Jersey	—	77
Johnson City, Tennessee	46	102
Chattanooga, Tennessee	30	107
Durham, North Carolina	19	140
High Point, North Carolina	50	157
Greensboro, North Carolina	25	170

The two groups were alike in size, but there was some difference in location. There was a larger number of decreasing cities in New England and a larger number of increasing cities in the Middle West. This fact has to be borne in mind in interpreting the differences, for some of the differences between these two groups may be due to regional differences rather than to rates of increase or decrease.

One further point of method. The differences that do appear may be due not to rates of growth and decline but rather to economic differences, since the growing cities usually have more economic opportunities than decreasing ones. But there seems no way of untangling this relationship between economic opportunity and growth. It is also true to a certain extent that cities which are growing faster are on the average a little younger, but this factor should not be very much of a disturbance in the comparisons.

ECONOMIC CONDITIONS

A growing population means generally an increasing local market, hence the established businesses are favored. Those that manufacture and those that sell like very much to see the population increase. Indeed the census rolls for particularly ambitious cities have been known to be padded with false names. But since the variation in the increase of most cities is generally due more to migration than to excess of births over deaths, the newcomers must be attracted for some reason, which is often economic. The average annual earnings in manufacturing are $1,250 in the increasing cities and $1,210 in the declining ones, and $1,330 in retail stores in the increasing cities, as compared with $1,320 in the decreasing cities—not much difference. But the slightly larger per cent paying income taxes is in the growing cities, 6.9 per cent to 6.6 per cent in the decreasing ones.

Again the difference may be due to the small number of cases. But the per cent of families having radios is 45 in the growing cities compared to 41 per cent in the decreasing ones. The rent paid is higher in the growing cities, $29.50 a month as compared with $23.30 in the decreasing cities. But the rent paid is probably not in this case a very good criterion of the incomes of the two places, for in places where people are moving out, vacancies should reduce rents, and similarly it may be questioned whether new building keeps pace with a growing population. If it does, the future values may be capitalized into present prices. The average value of the house and lot reported to the census was $5,500 in the decreasing cities and $5,700 in the increasing ones. While the differences in these various economic factors are slight, taken together they increase the probability that at the present time the economic conditions are more favorable in the growing cities. This differential will probably exist in the future even if the slowing up of population growth becomes general.

OCCUPATIONS

There seems to be no good theory which would indicate any reason why one occupation should be more frequent in a growing city than in a decreasing one. The increasing cities have a slightly larger percentage of their working population in trade, 16 as compared with 13 in the decreasing cities. Also they have a slightly smaller per cent in manufacturing, 43 as compared with 46. But these may be regional differences. The cities of the Northeast for instance have large percentages in manufacturing and small percentages in trade. On the other hand there may be technological rather than regional reasons for a decrease in the population of certain manufacturing centers. The percentages of the employed population that are physicians are larger in the increasing cities, .38 per cent as compared with .29. The same difference is noted as regards lawyers, .35 as compared with .27. Perhaps the lawyers and physicians are quick to follow population changes. It seems probable that if adequate data existed for a variety of detailed occupations, differences would show up, but the gross figures show little difference.

POPULATION

There are more young adults and middle-aged adults in the increasing cities. This population difference is to be expected as it is a characteristic of migration in modern times. This migration leaves the old people in the decreasing places which the young leave. There are also more young people under 20 years of age in the decreasing cities. This seems also in accord with the theory that the families with children do not migrate as readily as those without.

Any differences between growing and decreasing cities in regard to the foreign-born

and the native stock would seem to be accidental. That is, there should be no inherent relationship between growth and place of birth. But in the cities here studied the percentage of the population that is native-born

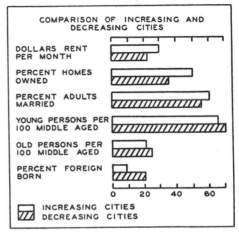

White of native stock is almost twice as great in the increasing cities. The sample of decreasing cities comes more largely from New England where there are a great many foreign-born. Yet the differences are extreme; 21 per cent of the decreasing populations are foreign-born White but only 9 per cent of the increasing populations.

FAMILY

The percentage married is definitely greater in the increasing cities, 61 per cent of those 15 years of age and over, as compared with 56 per cent in the decreasing cities. This difference is in part due to the influence of New England and of the presence of large numbers of the offspring of the foreign-born. Both of these influences discourage marriage. Still the difference is quite large, and the economic factor is likely to be one to encourage marriage in the growing city. It seems reasonable to think that the influences found in decreasing populations may discourage marriage somewhat.

The percentage widowed is greater in the decreasing cities, 8.4 per cent in comparison with 7.6 per cent in the increasing cities. The explanation may be due in part to the reluctance of older people, from which group the widowed come, to move to new places. On the other hand the percentages of single men 20 to 35 years old is greater in the decreasing cities, as is true also of the women of that age who have never married. They should be freer to migrate perhaps, but their greater numbers in the decreasing cities may be due to influences affecting marriage.

There does not seem to be much difference in the size of the family. It may be that opposing forces of economic conditions and migrating tendencies cancel each other. The number of little children is slightly larger in the cities that are decreasing, which may be due to influences of religion or of location rather than to rates of population change. One would expect the decreasing cities to have lower birth rates, of course.

As to the economic indices of family life there are several differences. More families with boarders and lodgers, 12 per cent, are found in the increasing cities, while in the decreasing cities there are only 9 per cent. At the same time there are more hotel keepers in the cities increasing in population. This may mean more new arrivals who have not yet set up homes. At the same time there seem to be slightly more persons engaged in personal and domestic service. There are also more married women employed outside the home in the growing cities. All these aspects of family life seem to be related to growing populations.

Another characteristic concerns the woman as head of a family. When a woman is head, she is usually a widow or separated from her husband. In the cities with decreasing populations 18 per cent of the families have a woman as head, while in the cities with increasing populations only 14 per cent of the families have women as heads. This difference may be due to the migration of men more than women away from the decreasing cities. In some rapidly growing cities there are more married men than married women.

Another interesting observation concerns renters and home owners, the latter being more frequent in the cities growing rapidly, where one-half the families live in homes which they own. In the decreasing cities only

a little over a third live in their own homes. It seems probable that the expectation of rising real estate values may encourage the ownership of homes in these cities with increasing populations. A home is a better investment there than in a decreasing city (see Table 3).

In conclusion, then, it is shown that economic advantages are slightly superior in the cities which are growing rapidly in population. Also the population of increasing cities is more concentrated in the ages that are income producing and hence there are fewer

TABLE 3

TRAITS OF INCREASING AND DECREASING CITIES

SOCIAL CHARACTERISTICS	INCREASING CITIES	DECREASING CITIES
Teachers per 100 Workers	2.27	2.25
Clergymen	.32	.27
Police	.29	.41
Hotel and Restaurant Keepers	.23	.19
Personal and Domestic Service Workers	12.20	11.26
Factory Workers	42.93	45.71
Trade Workers	15.62	12.97
Radios, % of Families Owning	45.0	41.0
Income Taxpayers, % of Adults	6.78	6.57
Median Monthly Rental	29.5	23.3
Median Value of Homes	5,700	5,537
Annual Earnings Rate, Mfg	1,250	1,210
Annual Earnings Rate, Retail	1,330	1,320
Married, % of Adults	61.0	56.0
Widowed, % of Adults	7.6	8.4
Median Size of Family, Minus Families of One	3.51	3.57
Children under Five Per 100 Married Women	56.3	59.3
Families With No Young Children in %	59.0	62.0
Married Women Employed, in %	30.0	25.7
Home Owners, % of Families	50.0	36.4
Apartment Houses, % of Dwellings	2.0	8.4
Families With Lodgers, in %	12.30	9.45
Sex Ratio of Single Men to Single Women	113.0	113.7
Single Men, 20-35, in %	15.0	16.3
Single Women, 20-35, in %	11.5	12.4
Debt Per Capita	107.0	92.1
Taxes Per Capita	42.40	55.84
Native Whites of Native Parents, in %	65.0	36.0
Foreign-born Whites, in %	9.0	21.0
School Attendance at 16-17 in %	57.0	54.5
Young Persons as Ratio to Middle Aged	.67	.71
Old Persons as Ratio to Middle Aged	.22	.25
Children, 10-15, Employed, in %	2.3	2.3
21 Years of Age and under, in %	37.5	38.3

that do not earn and have to be supported. This age distribution favors a good economic situation for there are fewer burdens of dependents among young and old. Indeed most of the other social characteristics that are peculiar to increasing and to decreasing cities seem to be related to these two factors of increased opportunity for income and migration. These other associated phenomena are, however, interesting on their own account and seem to indicate the basis for a more optimistic spirit in the growing cities.

CHAPTER XIV

GOVERNMENT AND POPULATION CHANGES

City governments are slow to keep up with population changes. In many departments per capita costs are greater in cities that are decreasing in population.

IN studying the characteristics of increasing and decreasing cities, it was noticed that there were more police in the cities that were losing population than in those which were gaining population, when the cities were the same size and in other respects similar. Thus in a sample of decreasing cities described previously there were 413 policemen per 100,000 of the working population in contrast to 285 policemen in cities that were gaining population. There are thus about 45 per cent more police in the decreasing cities than in the increasing cities. Why should this be? Is there more crime in cities that are declining? Probably not. It would seem that there is just as much reason to think crime would flourish more in a rapidly growing city. There seems to be no reason why the traffic regulations should be different in the two types of places.

When the matter was viewed from the budgetary point of view, it was found that the cost of the police department in the cities with a declining population was about 50 per cent greater than the cost in a rapidly growing city, other non-governmental factors being approximately equal. It was further observed that when a city is growing rapidly the economic conditions are more favorable than in a city growing less rapidly or than in a decreasing city. Hence a growing city could seem better able to afford a larger police force than a decreasing city.

Further reflection recalls that budgets are made up the year previous for the year following. Now, in the year previous the population is smaller in a growing city than it is in the succeeding year. If budgets should be made out on the basis of the past year rather than on the probable population needs of the future year it is easy to see how the number of police would be few. It is common enough, of course, for human beings to look backward instead of forward. It is perhaps even more common for governments to do the same thing. Hence failure to anticipate the future needs of a growing population may be the explanation of the small number of police in the growing city, just as cities fail to anticipate the needs of a future population in planning parks and wide streets.

On the other side the same forces may work in the opposite direction for the cities which are losing population. The possible loss of population is not anticipated. Indeed, the city is loath to admit such a trend. Police requirements based on the past may then be more than are necessary for the requirements of a smaller future population. There are, no doubt, other considerations that make a city slow to adjust its police force to the needs of a changing population. For instance, police have tenure of office and they are provided with pension funds in many cities. Then it may be difficult to reduce a governmental force of this nature.

It would seem then that the government of a growing city and the government of a decreasing city are slow in making adjustments to their changing populations. If this explanation be the correct one, we are curious to know whether the same phenomenon is noticeable in regard to other governmental expenditures. Accordingly, recourse was had to the records and the following results were noted regarding other bureaus and departments.

The costs of the fire department like the costs of the police department are more in the communities that are shrinking in population. Indeed, the difference is even greater, about 65 per cent more per capita. Here there are property considerations as truly as population requirements.

The cost per capita of the street cleaning department is nearly twice as great in the cities with decreasing populations. That the cost might be somewhat greater is clear since it may be determined by the mileage of streets rather than by the population. Still so great an increase hardly seems explained since the mileage is probably nearly the same.

The lighting of streets costs only a very little more per capita in the decreasing cities. Perhaps the labor cost is not so large a part of total costs in this department and the lighting of streets may be called for whether there are few or many living on a street.

The care of parks and trees is about 50 per cent greater in costs per capita in the decreasing cities. In this case it may be that the rapidly growing city has not laid out as much park and boulevard space as in the older cities.

A very interesting item is the cost of inspection of buildings, wiring, plumbing, boilers, etc. The cost per capita is about 50 per cent greater in the decreasing city than in the growing city. However, there would seem to be more inspection needed in the growing city presumably because of more building construction to care for the incoming population. The care of sewers and sewage disposal is slightly more costly in the decreasing city, though there is no apparent reason why this should be so.

Also the departmental budget for food regulations and the inspection of food is a good deal greater in the decreasing city. The labor item is no doubt large in this budget.

In regard to education the cost of schools per adult 21 years of age and over is about 20 per cent greater per capita in the cities that are losing population, although wages in general are lower. There are, though,

more children in these cities in comparison to the adults than there are in the growing cities, and so for this reason there is some justification for more expenditure per adult supporting the schools. However, it is true that the cost of the schools per pupil is also greater in cities that are losing population. Though there are more children in the declining cities, the percentage of children 16 and 17 years old attending school is less. It is difficult to see why the school costs per child should be greater in the decreasing cities.

The cost of libraries per capita like the school costs is less in the cities with increasing populations. Why the reading habits in the two types of cities should be different is not clear.

The amount of money spent per capita on the conservation of health is much greater in the decreasing cities, more than twice as much. The cost of medical service for children is about 40 per cent greater.

The most striking difference found is in the expenditures on charities. The per capita expenditures in the declining cities are over five times as great. Why there should be so very great a difference here is not known. Perhaps the economic conditions are much less favorable.

The only exceptions to this general conclusion that were found were possibly two. One was the budget for the department of roads which was a little larger in the rapidly growing cities. Perhaps roadways in a growing city require very much more money spent on them. The other exception was the amount of money spent on the provision of public recreation which was a fraction greater in the increasing cities. In these two cases the differences were so slight that they were hardly significant for the number of cities studied, which was 41, 20 in one sample and 21 in the other.

Finally, when the total general governmental expenditures were compared, it was found that they were greater in the declining cities—only about 15 per cent greater however, not as much difference as in the special departmental budgets reported above.

This brief survey of governmental expenditures shows that in many different departments the costs per capita are greater when the populations are decreasing. That is to say, the difference is hardly to be explained by peculiarities within all these different departments. A more general explanation common to them all is needed. This is what is done by the theory set forth in the beginning of this article, accounting for the greater police force in the decreasing cities.

The theory is that governments of increasing cities do not anticipate in actual budgeting practice the needs of the larger future populations and that the governments of decreasing cities do not anticipate in practice the diminished needs of smaller future populations. As to why governments do not make these budgetary adjustments more quickly, there may be many other reasons than mere inertia. They may have obligations to their employees; they may be justified in proceeding slowly until the needs of

the population are shown; there may be possibilities of abuse if budgets are constructed on too hypothetical considerations. But the fact remains that city governments are slow to keep up with population changes. Slowness of governments to adjust themselves to technological changes has been discussed elsewhere.[1] It was there stated that the technological change came first and that only later, after a considerable lag, did the government change to keep up with the advancing technology. In this special consideration of governmental behavior in increasing and in decreasing cities, it is population, not technology, which changes first, to be followed after a lag by action in the various governmental departments.

---

[1]William F. Ogburn, "Technology and Governmental Change," *Journal of Business*, Vol. IX, January, 1936.

INDEX

Actors and showmen, 9
Ages: ratio young to middle, 2, 29, 38, 49, 53, 58, 59, 63, 64; ratio old to middle, 2, 29, 31, 38, 49, 53, 58, 59, 63, 64
Apartment houses, 15, 39, 49, 53, 59, 64
Artists, 9, 31
Assault, 10
Authors, 59
Automobile theft, 10
Average city, how it was found, 36

Birth rate, 2, 29, 64
Births and deaths, 2
Burglary, 10

Charities and correction, 17, 18, 30, 67
Children: young, 12, 31, 49, 53, 58, 59, 64; employed, 14, 31, 49, 53, 64
Church membership, 9, 10, 30, 31
Classes, size of city, 1
Cleaning, dyeing and pressing, 15, 16
Clergy, 9, 10, 37, 49, 53, 57, 59, 64
Clerical, 7, 37, 57, 59
College town, 46
Communication, *See* transportation
Cost of living, 4
Courts and police, 20, 30, 49, 53
Criminal occupations, 10

Death rate, 2, 3, 29
Debt: city, 21, 40, 49, 53, 59, 64; ratio to value of city property, 21
Decreasing cities, 61
Dentists, 8
Domestic service, 7, 11, 15, 37, 38, 49, 53, 57, 59, 64
Dwellings: size of, 22; age of, 22, 23; facilities of, 22, 23; length of occupation, 23, 24; overcrowded, 22, 23

Economic conditions, 15, 52, 62
Education: costs per adult, 19, 59, 67; per child, 19, 59, 67
Electricians, 15, 31, 59
Employment, 14
Expenditures, consumers, 24, 25

Factory towns, 42
Factory workers, *See* manufacturing
Families: 11, 52, 58, 63; size of, 11, 12, 30, 39, 49, 53, 59, 64; with lodgers, 11, 12, 30, 49, 53, 59, 64; with servants, 11; with no young children, 12, 39, 49, 53, 59; with many children, 12; with women head, 13, 14, 64; with gainful workers, 14, 30, 39, 59
Fire department, cost of, 67
Foreign born, 3, 29, 38, 49, 53, 57, 59, 63

Government, 20, 29, 30, 54, 59, 67

Hairdressers, 59
Health, conservation of, 18, 30, 49, 53, 67
Health resorts, 45
Homes: value of, 4, 5, 39, 49, 53, 59, 62; rental of, 4, 5, 29, 39, 49, 53, 59, 62; owned, 15, 16, 30, 39, 49, 53, 59, 63
Hospitals, 26
Hotel: expenditures, 15; keepers, 49, 53, 64

Increasing cities, 62
Incomes and cost of living, 4
Income taxpayers, 64
Inspection of buildings, and food, 67

Larceny, 10
Lawyers, 8, 29, 37, 57, 59, 63
Leisure, 26
Librarians, 19, 20
Libraries, 19, 31, 49, 53, 59, 67

Major classes of population, the, 6
Manslaughter, 10
Manufacturing, 6, 29, 37, 57, 59, 63, 64
Marital status: married, 13, 39, 49, 53, 58, 59, 63; single, 13, 39, 49, 53, 64; widowed, 13, 14, 29, 39, 49, 53, 58, 59, 63
Marriage, 12
Men and women, 3
Middlewestern cities, characteristics of, 30
Mining towns, 44
Murder, 10
Museums, 27
Musicians, 9, 31, 37, 57, 59

Native white: of foreign parentage, 3, 38; of native parentage, 3, 38, 57, 59, 63
Negroes, 29, 37, 38
Northeastern cities, characteristics of, 29

Occupations, 52, 57, 63
Opera, 27
Orchestras, 26

Pacific Coast cities, characteristics of, 31
Parks and trees, cost of, 67
Personal service, *See* domestic service
Physicians, 8, 29, 37, 57, 59, 63
Pleasure resorts, 45
Professions, 7, 8, 29, 37, 57, 59
Police, *See* courts
Policemen, 20, 37, 49, 53, 59, 64, 66
Population characteristics, 57, 63
Public utilities, 20
Public service, 57, 59

METROPOLITAN AMERICA

AN ARNO PRESS COLLECTION

Adams, Thomas. **The Design of Residential Areas:** Basic Considerations, Principles, and Methods. (Harvard City Planning Studies, Vol. VI). 1934.

Anderson, Wilbert L. **The Country Town:** A Study of Rural Evolution. 1906.

Arnold, Bion J. **Report on the Improvement and Development of the Transportation Facilities of San Francisco.** Submitted to the Mayor and the Board of Supervisors, City of San Francisco. March, 1913. 1913.

Association for the Improvement of the Condition of the Poor. **Housing Conditions in Baltimore.** Report of a Special Committee of the Association for the Improvement of the Condition of the Poor and the Charity Organization Society. Submitting the Results of an Investigation Made by Janet E. Kemp. 1907.

Bassett, Edward M. **Zoning:** The Laws, Administration, and Court Decisions During the First Twenty Years. 1936.

Bauer, Catherine. **Modern Housing.** 1934.

Case, Walter H. **History of Long Beach and Vicinity.** (Volume 1). 1927.

Chamberlin, Everett. **Chicago and Its Suburbs.** 1874.

Chapin, E[dwin] H[ubbell]. **Humanity in the City.** 1854.

Coit, Stanton. **Neighborhood Guilds:** An Instrument of Social Reform. 1891.

Comey, Arthur C[oleman]. **Transition Zoning.** (Harvard City Planning Studies, Vol. V). 1933.

Covington, Kentucky, City Planning and Zoning Commission. **Comprehensive Plan for Covington, Kentucky, and Environs.** [1932].

Goodnow, Frank J. **City Government in the United States.** 1910.

Hinman, Albert Greene. **Population Growth and Its Demands Upon Land for Housing in Evanston, Illinois.** 1931.

Hubbard, Theodora Kimball and Henry Vincent Hubbard. **Our Cities To-Day and To-Morrow:** A Survey of Planning and Zoning Progress in the United States. 1929.

Kellogg, Paul Underwood, editor. **The Pittsburgh District Civic Frontage** (Pittsburgh Survey, Vol. 5). 1914.

Kellogg, Paul Underwood, editor. **Wage-Earning Pittsburgh** (Pittsburgh Survey, Vol. 6). 1914.

Knowles, Morris. **Industrial Housing:** With Discussion of Accompanying Activities; Such as Town Planning, Street Systems, Development of Utility Services, and Related Engineering and Construction Features. 1920.

Lindsey, Ben B. and Rube Borough. **The Dangerous Life.** 1931.

Marsh, Benjamin Clarke. **An Introduction to City Planning:** Democracy's Challenge to the American City. With a Chapter on the Technical Phases of City Planning by George B. Ford. [1909].

Maxwell, Sidney D. **The Suburbs of Cincinnati:** Sketches, Historical and Descriptive. 1870.

Metropolitan Police Manuals—1871, 1913. Introduction by Richard C. Wade. 1974.

Moehlman, Arthur B. **Public Education in Detroit.** 1925.

National Municipal League. Committee on Metropolitan Government. **The Government of Metropolitan Areas in the United States.** Prepared by Paul Studenski with the Assistance of the Committee on Metropolitan Government. 1930.

National Resources Committee. **Our Cities:** Their Role in the National Economy. Report of the Urbanism Committee to the National Resources Committee. 1937.

New York City. Board of Aldermen. Committee on General Welfare. **Preliminary Report of the Committee on General Welfare in the Matter of a Request of the Conference of Organized Labor Relative to Educational Facilities.** Meeting of June 26, 1917. 1917.

New York City. Staten Island Improvement Commission. **Report of a Preliminary Scheme of Improvements.** 1871.

Ogburn, William F. **Social Characteristics of Cities:** A Basis for New Interpretations of the Role of the City in American Life. 1937.

Pink, Louis H. **The New Day in Housing.** 1928.

Powell, Hickman. **Ninety Times Guilty.** 1939.

Regional Plan Association. **From Plan to Reality.** 1933/1938/1942. 3 volumes in one.

Regional Plan of New York and Its Environs. 2 volumes. 1929/1931.

Regional Survey of New York and Its Environs. 10 volumes. 1927-1931.

Simonds, Thomas C. **History of South Boston;** Formerly Dorchester Neck, Now Ward XII of the City of Boston. 1857.

Smythe, William E. **City Homes on Country Lanes:** Philosophy and Practice of the Home-in-a-Garden. 1921.

Straus, Nathan. **The Seven Myths of Housing.** 1944.

Studies of Suburbanization in Connecticut. Numbers 1-3. 1936/1938/1939.

Toulmin, Harry Aubrey, Jr. **The City Manager:** A New Profession. 1916.

U.S. Public Health Service. **Municipal Health Department Practice for the Year 1923.** Based Upon Surveys of the 100 Largest Cities in the United States Made by the United States Public Health Service in Cooperation with the Committee on Administrative Practice, American Public Health Association. Public Health Bulletin No. 164. 1926.

U.S. Senate. Committee on the District of Columbia. **City Planning.** Hearing Before the Committee on the District of Columbia, United States Senate, on the Subject of City Planning. 61st Congress, 2nd Session, Senate Document No. 422. 1910.

U.S. Senate. Juvenile Court of the District of Columbia. **Message from the President of the United States Transmitting a Letter from the Judge of the Juvenile Court of the District of Columbia Submitting a Report Covering the Work of the Juvenile Court During the Period From July 1, 1906, to June 30, 1926.** 69th Congress, 2nd Session, Senate Document No. 236. 1927.

Upson, Lent D. **Practice of Municipal Administration.** 1926.

West Side Studies. Carried on Under the Direction of Pauline Goldmark. 1914. 2 volumes in one.

Wilcox, Delos F[ranklin]. **Great Cities in America:** Their Problems and Their Government. 1910.

Zueblin, Charles. **American Municipal Progress.** 1916.